Com
Ja

tweet treats

140 characters, 140 celebrities, recipes for every occasion

THE O'BRIEN PRESS
DUBLIN

Jane Travers has a BA in English and an MA in Film Studies from UCD. These days, she makes stuff up and writes it down, and exists in deep denial about her addiction to Twitter. She lives in Kildare, Ireland with her endlessly patient husband and daughter, who acted as guinea pigs for many of the *Tweet Treats* recipes. She is often to be found walking her dogs on the Curragh and muttering to herself.

Dedication

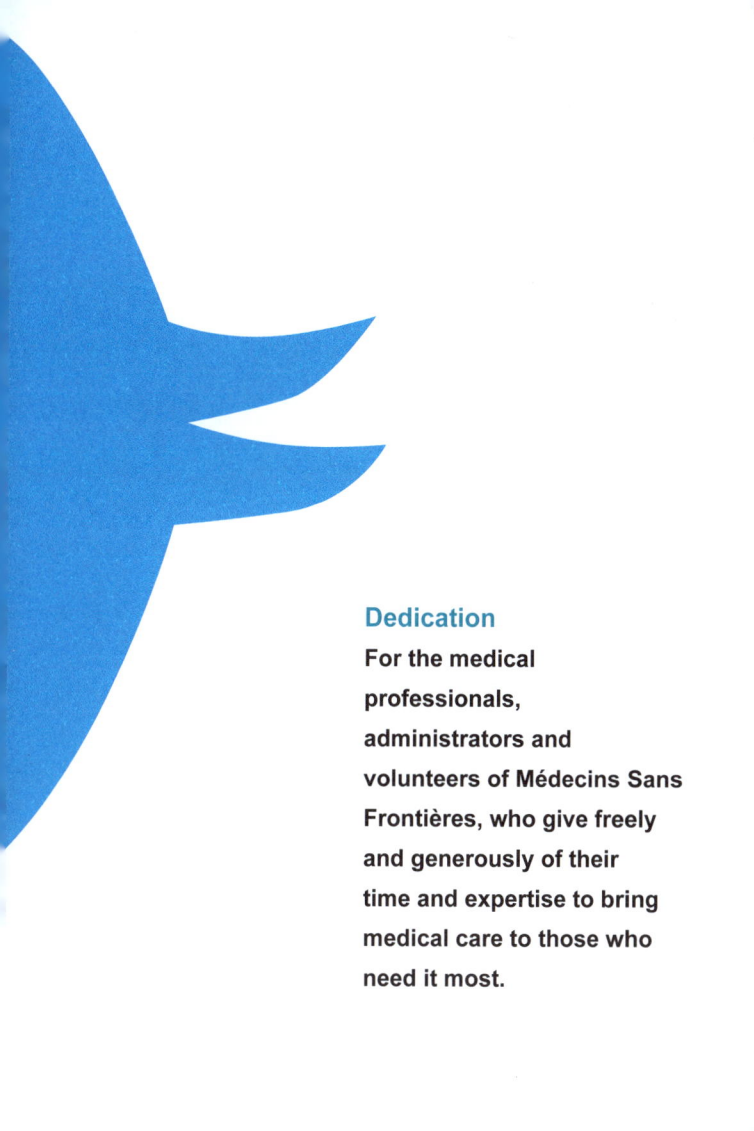

For the medical professionals, administrators and volunteers of Médecins Sans Frontières, who give freely and generously of their time and expertise to bring medical care to those who need it most.

First published 2011 by The O'Brien Press Ltd,
12 Terenure Road East,
Rathgar,
Dublin 6,
Ireland.
Tel: +353 1 4923333;
Fax: +353 1 4922777
E-mail: books@obrien.ie
Website: www.obrien.ie

ISBN: 978-1-84717-302-7

Tweeted recipes copyright © individual tweeters, included with their permission.
Introduction copyright © Marco Pierre White.
All other text copyright © Jane Travers.
Copyright for typesetting, layout, editing, design
© The O'Brien Press Ltd

All rights reserved.
No part of this publication may be reproduced
or utilised in any form or by any means,
electronic or mechanical, including photocopying,
recording or in any information storage
and retrieval system, without permission
in writing from the publisher.

A catalogue record for this title is available from the British Library

1 2 3 4 5 6 7 8
11 12 13 14 15

Printed and bound by GraphyCEMS
The paper used in this book is produced using pulp from managed forests

Kindly sponsored by Knorr

Contents

Foreword by Marco Pierre White	6
Introduction by Médecins Sans Frontières	8
Acknowledgements	10
Glossary	**12**
Breakfast	**14**
Snacks & Sides	**25**
Sandwiches	**37**
Salads & Dressings	**49**
Soups & Sauces	**60**
Fish	**72**
Perfect Poultry	**82**
Meat	**93**
Pasta & Rice Dishes	**104**
Vegetarian & Vegan Dishes	**117**
Spreads, Dips & Preserves	**128**
Sweet Tweet Treats	**139**
Desserts	**146**
Cakes & Bakes	**163**
Party Food	**175**
Drinks	**184**
Cooking Tips by Marco Pierre White	**195**
'Food Inspired by the Movies' Quiz	**196**

Foreword

The love of food is universal. All over the world people come together to socialise while they eat, whether over a leisurely four-course dinner or a hastily-thrown-together meal at the end of the working day.

I believe that food should be simple. There's no need to make life difficult with complicated recipes and fiddly ingredients when you can do so much with basics like ***Knorr*** stock cubes in your cupboard. I would like everyone to know a few quick recipes that can be adapted depending on what's in the fridge. Even without much technical ability you can still cook dinner for your friends and family and have a sense of occasion, which I believe is important.

Cooking should be a pleasure, not a chore, but it is increasingly difficult to find the time to spend on good food for family and friends. In my book *Marco Made Easy* I say, 'It'll take you less time to make the dishes than to wash them'. Well, in *Tweet Treats* it will take you less time to read the recipes than it would take to pour yourself a glass of wine! This book really is the love of food pared down to its bones; simple recipes, delicately expressed – just as you would convey a recipe in a conversation with a friend.

Nourishing ourselves with lovingly-prepared food does us all good, but this book is doing good in other ways too in its support of the fantastic charity Médecins Sans Frontières. In buying this book you are spreading the love of simple food and spreading medical help to those who need it. I wish *Tweet Treats* the very best of luck.

Marco Pierre White

Introduction by Médecins Sans Frontières

Jane Travers first contacted Médecins Sans Frontières in Dublin in May 2010 to see if we would accept all the royalties from a recipe book, to be called *Tweet Treats*. As fundraising ideas go, it was certainly unique. But considering that we weren't entirely clear on the difference between a hash tag and a hash brown, we weren't quite sure what to think initially.

However upon meeting with Jane, we were quickly won over. Her creativity, energy and genuine support for the work of Médecins Sans Frontières were infectious, and it was obvious that any project she committed to would be a success. The elements that make Twitter so effective – its immediacy, its international scope – are the same things that make Médecins Sans Frontières a leader in the field of humanitarian medical aid.

Médecins Sans Frontières this year celebrates the 40th anniversary of its creation by a group of doctors and journalists to provide independent humanitarian medical aid wherever needed, and to speak out against suffering. Our volunteers, including those from the UK and Ireland, have worked in countries from Afghanistan to Haiti to Zimbabwe providing emergency medical aid to people most in need. With the support and generosity of the public, and with great fundraising initiatives such as *Tweet Treats* we can continue to respond to medical emergencies, whenever and wherever needed.

We'd like to extend our huge thanks to Jane for creating *Tweet Treats* and driving the project through to this wonderful conclusion. We'd also like to thank everyone who contributed a recipe. Finally, we'd like to thank you for your support in purchasing this book. To find out more about our work and how we're spending your money, visit www.msf.ie or www.msf.org.uk. And you can follow us on Twitter: @MSF_ireland and @MSF_uk

Sophie Chaix
Head of Office
Médecins Sans Frontières/
Doctors Without Borders (MSF) Ireland
June 2011

Acknowledgements

Many writers refer to their books as their 'babies'; that's definitely how I feel about *Tweet Treats*, so when I originally came up with the idea and floated it on Twitter, I felt like an anxious parent sending her child out into the world to make its own way. To take the analogy further, it takes a village to raise a child, and it certainly took an entire on-line community to nurture *Tweet Treats* to maturity.

Every single person mentioned in these pages has given of their time and their brain power to craft perfect little recipes in 140 characters or less. I thank them all, but some deserve special mention. The self-allocated #teamtweettreats banded together to ask as many celebrities as possible to contribute. Huge thanks go to @rebeccaebrown, @Chiddle84, @thejayfaulkner, @ShirtNTie, @LevParikian, @Cathyby and mother/daughter team @NettieWriter and @clairecatrina (the youngest contributor to the book). A very special mention goes to celeb-slut extraordinaire @mduffywriter who discovered a rather scary talent for interacting with celebrities and bringing them round to her way of thinking!

All the celebrities who contributed did so with great warmth, generosity of spirit and good humour. I am awed and gratified by their interest and good wishes.

@neversarah gave awesome professional advice and is generally wonderful. @inkwellHQ (also @writing_ie) guided, advised, mentored, pushed, prodded and shoved me and I couldn't be more grateful to her.

Michael O'Brien of The O'Brien Press saw what a little gem *Tweet Treats* was, and handed me over to @HelenOBP, editor and organised person extraordinaire. Huge thanks to them and to all at The O'Brien Press. I'm also enormously grateful to my agent, @sallyanne_s of @watsonlittle, for her time and expertise.

Sincere thanks have to go to the amazing Marco Pierre White, who donated the foreword to this book. ***Knorr*** have very generously sponsored the book, thanks to Judy Fusco and Niamh O'Grady in ***Knorr*** for all their help.

Thanks to my family and friends who put up with a lot of talk about this project for over a year, with varying degrees of amusement, bemusement and confusion. But most of all, thanks to my beloved husband @ukegnome and my 'dd' Lia, who've had their fill of *Tweet Treats* in more ways than one! Love you, guys.

Glossary

• • • • • • • • • • • • • • • • • •

Because the *Tweet Treats* recipes are so short, you'll find they are gently sprinkled with abbreviations. These have been kept to a minimum to allow the recipes to be as instantly readable and accessible as possible. Many of them will be familiar to you already, such as:

tsp	teaspoon	**kg**	kilograms
dsp	dessert spoon	**ml**	millilitres
tbsp	table spoon	**L**	litres
g	grams	**cm**	centimetres

All weights and measurements in the book are metric. The only other abbreviations you will encounter are:

w	with	**EVOO**	extra virgin olive oil
&	and	**FR**	free range
S&P	salt and pepper	**F-ch**	finely-chopped
OO	olive oil	**Bak pwdr**	baking powder

For all recipes that require baking/roasting, a pre-heated oven is assumed.

All oven temperatures are in Celsius (centigrade), which can be converted here as follows:

140c	280F	Gas 1-2
160c	320F	Gas 3
180c	350F	Gas 4
190c	375F	Gas 5
200c	400F	Gas 6
220c	425F	Gas 7
230c	450F	Gas 8
240c	475F	Gas 9

Each recipe in *Tweet Treats* is categorised using one or more of the following icons:

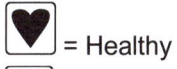

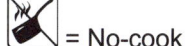

= Celebrity

= Professional

= Tip

= Funny

= Easy

= Quick

= Healthy

= Budget

= No-cook

= Vegan

= Vegetarian

Breakfast

Whether your usual choice of breakfast is a hasty bowl of cereal or a full fry, we all get bored occasionally and need some variety. On the following pages you'll find inspiration to shake up your first meal of the day, from quick and easy fruity recipes, to smoothies, to luxurious Sunday morning treats.

Breakfast is the most important meal of the day, but it's also the most hurried for most of us. If you don't have time to whip up a hollandaise sauce for Eggs Benedict – or even to boil an egg – you'll find breakfast ideas on the following pages that take minutes or even seconds to throw together, to get your day off to the right start.

Fruit Breakfasts:

[L] Blueberry Yogurt @janjonesauthor
Add a really generous handful of ripe blueberries to 150g cold Greek yogurt. Fold until smooth & thoroughly coated. Yum.
Award-winning author of Regency romance (including *The Kydd Inheritance*) and contemporary romantic comedy.

[L] Banana Maple Yogurt @SuzanneCollier
1 sliced banana, topped w fat-free fromage frais, maple syrup, handful of walnuts or hazelnuts, scrummy!

Tropical Breakfast @HazelKLarkin
1 ripe papaya, 1 fresh lime. Seed, peel & chop papaya. Squeeze lime juice over papaya. Eat. Yum.

Brilliant Berries @LevParikian
Raspberries & blackberries. Lemon juice squeezed over. Sugar sprinkled. A sprig of mint if you have it. Never mind if not.

Summer Brekkie @Candida6
Scoop 3 passion fruits, chop 1 banana, peel/stone mango, add 300ml orange juice and blitz, serve over ice.

Breakfast In A Glass @donalskehan
Blitz a handful of frozen berries with 1 banana and top with apple juice. Hey presto, a fab little breakfast smoothie!

Author of acclaimed cookbooks *Good Mood Food* & *Kitchen Hero*. Presents RTE's television cookery series, *Kitchen Hero*.

Oats So Good @fionamulreany
Soak 2tbsp porridge oats in apple juice for an hour. Top with natural yogurt and chopped fresh fruit. Fab breakfast and healthy!

TWEET TREATS 15

Slow Release Smoothie @lisamarie20010
Blend strawberries, bananas, natural yogurt and oats (also honey if you like it sweet) and drink as a breakfast smoothie.

Breakfast Stewed Apricots, Apples & Prunes @janetravers
Soak dried fruit in apple juice overnight. Into pan, add stick cinnamon & star anise. Stew until tender, reduce sauce. Serve with yogurt.

Poached Rhubarb @placepot
Rhubarb: wash & cube. Slow poach til soft, add ½tsp cinnamon, 1tsp of honey at end; very nice with yogurt.

Cereals

Granola @MichelleZink
300g oats, 40g chppd nuts, 90g dried fruit, ¼tsp coarse salt, 5tbsp mpl syrup, 5tsp oil, ½tsp vanilla. Bake @160c for 30 mins.
Michelle Zink, Author of the *Prophecy of the Sisters* Trilogy

Fruity Porridge @CountryLets
Boil 450ml watr, 1tbsp b/sugr,1tsp cinmn,2tbsp map/syrup. Lower heat, add 75g oats,stir 5min,remove from heat. Stir in apples,sultanas.Serve

Muesli @paulakahumbu
Mix equal amounts jumbo oats, rye, wheat, barley, sesame w sunflower & pumpkin seeds, hazel, brazil, walnuts, salt, honey. Slow roast, stir.
Paula Kahumbu, Ecologist, conservationist and children's author.

Pancakes & French Toast

Perfect Pancakes @andrea_mclean
Fave for me and kids: pancakes. 100g plain flour, 280ml milk, 1 egg, pinch of cinnamon. Whisk, spoon onto pan, fry. X
Andrea McLean, Popular Television presenter of ITV's *Loose Women*

Savoury Pancakes @PenguinGalaxy
When you flip pancake, sprinkle ham, cheese & parsley on top, this will cook as the other side of the pancake does. Roll up. Eat!

Gluten-Free Pancakes @bindiyayagnik
Dissolve lots of sugar into 120ml warm water & mix into 75g gram flour. Melt butter in pan, spoon mix on, fry pancakes.

Supertramp Pancakes @JackyHSF
Fry bacon strips, pour pancake batter over each strip, cook, flip, add maple syrup. Serve.

Dutchbaby @LOST_BOSS
100ml milk, 75g flour, 3 eggs, 1tbsp sugar, 1tsp vanilla. Melt 60g butter in cast-iron skillet, add batter. Bake 30 mins @ 190c till puffed. Lemon.

Basic French Toast @simiansuter
Wholemeal bread, sliced. Free range egg, beaten/seasoned. Immerse one in other. Remove & fry till both sides golden

Vanilla Toast @CountryLets
Mix 2 eggs, milk & 2tsp vanilla extract, soak white sliced bread 5 mins each side fry in butter&oil til brown, cover in sugar.

Marmalade French Toast @JackyHSF
Mix cream cheese & Cointreau marmalade. Sandwich 2 slices bread w 2tbsp mix. Dip in egg&milk mix. Fry, drizzle maple syrup, dash cinnamon.

Luxury French Toast @JackyHSF
Whisk: 1egg, 60g mltd buttr, 3tbsp sugar, 40g flour, ½ tsp ci'mon, pnch each n'meg, salt, 100ml milk, ¾ tsp vanilla. Dip brioche slices, fry.

Egg Dishes

Alan's Eggs @AlanCarr
Boil an egg for 4 mins, toast the bread, cut it into soldiers and dip into the runny yolk of the egg. Voila x
Stand up comedian and TV presenter

Luxury Scrambled Eggs @PenguinGalaxy
Put bits of smoked salmon with butter, cream and lots of fresh dill and black pepper into your scrambled eggs!

Baked Egg @RebeccaEmin
Grate cheddar into ramekin dish. Put an egg on top. Sprinkle w paprika. Bake in oven until egg cooked. Eat with toast.

Pakistani Eggs @SpiceSpoon
Caramelise onions, add chopped tomatoes. Pinch turmeric, salt, chilli powder. Crack eggs on top. Bake 15 mins at 180C.

Shakshuka @WineBlogIL
Fry 2 tomatoes & red pepper. Add 2 garlic cloves, salt & pepper. Break in 2 eggs & cook about 5 minutes. (Like huevos rancheros).

Rebus Roll @Beathhigh
Split a roll n toast inner surfaces. Fry an egg so it crisps at edges, but yolk stays soft. Red/brown sauce. Messy/delicious.

Ian Rankin, No. 1 best-selling crime author, creator of aclaimed 'Inspector Rebus' series.

Omelette @mruku
Chop and fry bacon, onion & mushrooms. When done spread evenly around pan and crack 4 eggs straight in. Fry until set. Scoff.

Mushroom Omelette @helen_kara
Beat eggs, stir in chopped mixed fresh herbs. Make omelette, top with fried mushrooms&garlic, grated cheese, pepper, fold over.

Bagel Holes @youngandfoodish
Drop knob of butter in fry pan. Drop half montreal sesame bagel in butter. Drop egg in hole. Heaven.

Spanish Eggs @goodtoweet
Lightly whisk 2 FR eggs, S&P. Cook low, stirring gently until just cooked. Add cubed, fried chorizo. Serve on buttered toast with chives.

Dreadful Breakfast @dreadfuls
Cut a circle from a square piece of toast & fry an egg in the hole. Dip the excess while considering futility of chickens.
British sketch-comedy troupe consisting of comedians Humphrey Ker, David Reed and Thom Tuck.

Dirty Eggs @mikelcu
Fry chopped tomatoes in a hot oiled frying pan. Use to garnish poached egg(s). Called 'dirty eggs' in spanish.

Love-It-Or-Loathe-It Brekkie @ukegnome
Toast rosemary and olive oil bread, cover in marmite, slice and dip into a big boiled egg... Don't eat in front of your wife!

Huevos Rotos ('Broken Eggs') @SCallejo
Slice potatoes into rounds, fry. Lay fried eggs over them on plate & then slices of serrano ham.

Pepper Rings @thornae
Fry egg inside slice/ring of green capsicum (bell pepper), serve on toasted muffin.

Brekkie Bagel @thescript
Whip egg in small bowl, thinly slice ham & tomato, add to the egg. Stick in microwave for 2 mins, put it between bagel halves!
Acclaimed chart-topping Irish alternative rock band The Script.

Super Scrambled Eggs for 2 @paulakahumbu
Whisk 4 eggs with 70ml milk, mix with 1 fried onion. Add 1tbsp f-ch parsley, 100g grated cheese, cook very slowly.
Paula Kahumbu, ecologist, conservationist and children's author.

Scrambled Egg in Nest @JackyHSF
Cut 3cm wide hole in thick slice bread. Rub on garlic. Fry in butter w egg (beaten with herbs) in hole. Season, Flip, Season.

Soda Bread Eggs @mduffywriter
Brown Soda Bread: Mix 400g each white & w'ml fl, tsp bread soda,salt,600ml buttr.milk. 45mins@200c.Cool. Slice.Hole in ctr.Fry egg in middle.

Claudia's Omelette @ClaudiaWinkle
Fry bacon and onions. Set aside. Whisk 2 eggs and grated cheddar. Mix all together and fry in pan. Add f-ch parsley. Yum.
Claudia Winkleman, British television presenter, radio personality and journalist

Other Cooked Breakfasts

Baldrick's Bun *Richard Curtis via @emmafreud*

Toasted bagel covered in cheese, grilled, smothered in baked beans, topped with crispy bacon. As delicious as. Richard Curtis is a screen writer, music producer, actor and film director, founder of Comic Relief. His partner Emma Freud is a script editor, producer, director of Red Nose Day and occasional broadcaster.

Kedgeree *@helen_kara*

Fry onion, add 1 part rice and 2 parts water, cover, simmer until cooked. Mix in tuna, chopped parsley, season. Add chopped hardboiled eggs.

Hush Puppies *@DazedPuckBunny*

Mix 2 beaten eggs, 55g sugar, 1 diced onion. Add 100g flour, 130g cornmeal, drop by tsp into 5cm oil at 180c, fry until golden.

Baked Tomatoes *@helen_kara*

Dot butter in bun tins. Put ½ tomato in each. Sprinkle with salt, pepper & dried herb(s) of choice. Bake. Better than fried.

Irish Potato Cakes @janetravers
Form cold, seasoned mashed potato into patties, roll in plain flour. Fry in half OO, half butter till golden both sides. Food of the gods!

Breakfast Pasta @illoydwebber
Hard boil an egg. Fry bacon. Boil pasta, drain. Add warm chopped egg, bacon. Mix with mayo...
Imogen Lloyd Webber, author/producer/liberal commentator for Fox News/MSN Life & Style Editor at Large

@helen_kara
For vegan fry-up, make bubble&squeak w olive oil, get vegan-friendly veggie sausages, add tomatoes/mushrooms/baked beans/toast Bubble & squeak see p 36

Roe on Toast @Cornflowerbooks
Dust herring roe with seasoned flour, sauté in butter til golden, serve on toast with squeeze of lemon. Wonderful!

Sherried Mushrooms on Toast @nicolamorgan
Fry sliced flat mushrooms, 2 splash sherry; reduce; add light crème fraiche; serve on toasted ciabatta w fresh coriander.
Nicola Morgan, award-winning author (of *Wasted* and others) & speaker re: books, teenage fiction, brains, publishing.

Snacks & Sides

You know how it is, it's too late for lunch but too early for dinner and you just want a little something to nibble on...

Snacks fill that gap between meals, keep hungry kids going until dinnertime or can be a treat in the evening. But there's no need to reach for the junk food when this chapter is jam-packed with tasty and appetising morsels. The beauty of these snacks is that many of them combine sweet with salty, satisfying all your cravings at once!

You'll also find great ideas for side dishes and starters to accompany and complement the fantastic main courses later in this book. If you've been guilty of serving frozen peas with every meal due to lack of inspiration, then read on!

Snacks

Easiest Snack Of All @arlenephillips
Frozen grapes!
Arlene Phillips, dancer, choreographer & popular judge on *Strictly Come Dancing.*

No Sour Grapes Here @helen_kara
Small seedless grape. Cover in soft blue cheese, shape into a ball. Roll in grated dark chocolate & eat. Go on, I dare you.

Haiku Food @SanyaV
Cubes of watermelon & feta cheese, mint leaves. Allow sweet & salty to conjugate in your mouth. Pink champagne.

L **V**

Banana Bundles @elainelarkin
Cut banana in half. Trim fat off a rasher. Wrap rasher around banana. Pin w a skewer. Grill/fry rasher as normal till cooked.

Posh Ploughmans @bahtocancer
1 plate. 1 slice Parma ham. 1 fig, quartered. 1 thin slice gorgonzola. A drizzle of hearty honey.

Figs In Prosciutto @LouDPhillips
Stem & halve Black Mission figs. Rub in EVOO. Sliver of parmesan. Fresh basil leaf. Wrap in prosciutto. Bake 180c 10 min or until crisp.

Lou Diamond Phillips, actor, writer & director of *Young Guns* & *La Bamba* fame.

Luxury Strawberry Snack @helen_kara
Fresh strawberries. Black pepper Boursin. Balsamic reduction if you wish; not essential. No cooking, just eat.

L

Melon & Parma Parcels @SanyaV
Wrap a slice of Parma ham around a slice of melon. Consume slowly. Sip champagne.

Perfection @LevParikian
Really good Stilton, a russet apple, walnuts. Maybe a glass of port. No need to muck around but take the time to savour flavours.

Moreish Cheese Balls @PositivelyBeaut
Mix 200g soft goat cheese, 10 finely-chopped black olives, S&P. Make 15 balls & roll in chopped pistachio nuts. Rejoice.

Alistair's Easiest Snack @campbellclaret
Two slices of toast in toaster. Open tin of beans. Cook beans on stove. Pour beans on toast when beanjuice sizzling. I don't cook!
Alistair Campbell, British journalist, broadcaster, political aide & author.

Roast Chickpeas @RhondaParrish
Open can of chickpeas. Rinse. Spread on baking sheet & drizzle w OO. Season w curry powder or seasoning salt. Bake 180c till crisp.

Roast Nuts @SanyaV
[V] Oven roast assorted nuts. Mix chopped fresh rosemary, muscovado sugar, salt, cayenne pepper, melted unsalted butter. Mix w nuts.

Aloo Tiki, Traditional Indian Snack @SarahTregear
[V] Mix mashed potato w breadcrumbs & chilli. Take handful, add frozen peas & chopped onion to centre. Mould into patty, fry until golden.

Movie Night Nachos @joannechocolat
Layer: big bag nacho chips, tin chopped tomatoes, chilli. Top w cheese. More chilli. Bake till cheese melts. Add Tarantino & serve!
Joanne Harris, multi-award winning & best-selling author of *Chocolat*, judge of the Whitbread & Orange prizes.

Stuffed Jalapeños @MarvinVAcuna
Halve & clean jalapeños. Mix small shrimp into bowl of cream cheese. Spoon into jalapeños, bake 10min & serve. Yummy!
Marvin Acuna, CEO & President of Rainmaker Films, AE Inc, Co-Founder of The Business of Show Institute

Bresaola With Rocket & Parmesan @SanyaV

Wrap rocket leaves & parmesan shavings into slice of bresaola. Savour. A light red in a glass.

Starters

Warm Artichoke Salad @MillaJovovich

Take artichoke, strip outer green & hair off. Cut in 4, fry in OO till brown. Put on lettuce, sprinkle w OO & parmesan!

Milla Jovovich, internationally-renowned actress & model, best known for her roles in *Resident Evil* & *The Fifth Element*

Warm Pear & Stilton Salad @helen_kara

Peel ripe pear. Leaving stalk intact, halve, core, slice, fan onto bed of watercress. Add slice(s) Stilton & grill very hot to melt.

Baked Peppers @JosaYoung

Halve sweet peppers, add anchovy, half tomato, slice sweet onion, OO, Herbes de Provence, season. Roast until singed.

Posh Cheese On Toast @Orbeeque

Thinly-cut slices of toasted Brioche covered w slices of goat's cheese & served w fresh figs makes a yummy starter.

Save Room For The Main Course
@rebeccaebrown

Melon chunks, halved grapes, finely-chopped ginger. Lovely fresh starter.

Side Dishes

Mustardy Cabbage *@loreleiking*
Fry 1tbsp mustard seeds in butter until they pop. Add chopped white cabbage. Cook on lowest heat until meltingly soft. Yum.

Lorelei King, Actress (*Cold Feet, Notting Hill, Emmerdale, Chef*), audiobook narrator, voiceover artist, writer.

A = Artichoke *@ElizabethBastos*
Steam six until tender, remove chokes, fill w holy trinity of garlic, OO & parmesan.

Lemon Garlic Glazed Corn On The Cob *@AllieDillon*
1tbsp butter, 1tbsp OO, 2 cloves minced garlic, 4 ears corn, 80ml water, 2tbsp lemon juice. Into a covered pan, gentle shake, steam 5-8mins.

Roast Beetroot *@goodtoweet*
Roast beetroot in packet of loose foil till tender, c45min. Cut into chunks. Dress in 3:1 EVOO & cider vinegar, S&P, fresh thyme while warm.

Spicy Cabbage @paulakahumbu
Lightly stir-fry 2 cups chopped cabbage, add ½ cup apple cider vinegar & 1tbsp sugar, 1tbsp chopped chilli, salt. Enjoy hot.
Paula Kahumbu, ecologist, conservationist & children's author.

Pea Purée @goodtoweet
Sweat ¼ onion in butter, add 100g cooked peas, S&P, squeeze of lemon juice. Blend until smooth, add handful chopped mint. Great w fish.

Celeriac Slaw @helen_kara
Grate celeriac. Dress w lemon juice, seedy mustard & mayo, mixed to taste. Serve w smoked trout.

Roast Fennel @goodtoweet
Toss 5mm thick slices fennel w EVOO, S&P, orange zest & chilli flakes. Roast on baking tray 180c 15mins or till tender.

Perfect Asparagus @janeaustenworld
Cut fresh thin asparagus stalks in 5cm lengths on the diagonal. Stir fry in OO & butter. Season w garlic salt. Serve.

TWEET TREATS

The Appetite Spoiler @Swannyg66
New old Trafford stand is worse than eating sprouts dipped in marmite. Washed down w turps.
Graeme Swann, English International cricketer.

@caroleagent
Asparagus must be fresh, pref organic. Steam *al dente* for shortest time possible – should still be crunchy. Terrible to steam to softness.

Chilli Plantain @helen_kara
Peel yellow plantain & slice diagonally 1-2 cm thick. Fry in hot oil till golden. Eat while still warm w chilli sauce.

Chilli Mango, Indian Side Dish @HazelKLarkin
1 green mango, 1tsp chilli powder, 1tsp salt. Half lime. Peel & chop mango. Sprinkle w chilli powder & salt. Squeeze lime over. Mix.

Eat Your Greens @HazelKLarkin
500g spinach, 7 cloves garlic, 1tsp harissa. Chop garlic, fry, add spinach & harissa, fry until spinach cooked (about 5 mins).

Orb Of Joy @SJRestaurant
Whole peeled red onions in dish. Add chick stock til almost covered (think icebergs) Medium oven, braise til cooked thru. Stock will glaze.
St. John Restaurant, est. by Fergus Henderson, author of *Nose to Tail Eating – a Kind of British Cooking* & Trevor Gulliver, noted restaurateur.

@SJRestaurant
Tip: Serve 1 Orb of Joy per person w a roasted chicken/partridge.
St. John Restaurant, est. by Fergus Henderson, author of *Nose to Tail Eating – a Kind of British Cooking* & Trevor Gulliver, noted restaurateur.

Dhal @helen_kara
Cook lentils w turmeric & sliced ginger. Fry onion seeds, sliced garlic & chilli in lots of ghee. Stir into lentils. Season.

Khicheri @JackyHSF
Heat 1tbsp oil. Cook pinch cumin seeds for 3 min. Add ½ cup yellow dhal, 1 cup cold rice. Cover w water. Cook till tender.

Yellow Cauli @PenguinGalaxy
Seethe garlic in butter in a frying pan. Then add blanched cauliflower, turmeric & lemon juice. Fry for a bit. Great veg!

TWEET TREATS

Meltingly Good Garlic @warrenellis
Make a strong pocket out of tinfoil. Slice the top off a head of garlic, throw garlic bulb in pocket, pour wine over, seal & roast 90 mins.

Warren Ellis, award-winning creator of graphic novels such as *Fell* & *Ministry of Space*, & the author of 'underground classic' *Crooked Little Vein*.

V **L**

Parsnip Bake @PositivelyBeaut
Boil then mash 3 parsnips, add 1tbsp mustard, 3 sprigs thyme, 150ml cream, 1 egg, S&P, nutmeg. Bake 180c until golden.

Baked Butternut @savorandcrave
Simplicity is best for certain veggies. For a quick side dish, brush honey-infused butter on butternut squash halves, oven roast or grill. For honey butter see page 131.

L

Butter Garlic Peas @BuddingGourmet
In a little butter, sauté some garlic, add fresh boiled peas & steam a bit.

L

Garlic Roast Potatoes @Chiddle84
1tbsp oil, S&P, lots of rosemary, oodles of garlic, toss potatoes in mix & roast for 30 mins. Brush teeth.

V **L**

Potato Rosti @heatherofficial
Grate 1 potato, ½ carrot, ½ parsnip, dash lemon, parsley, oil, S&P. Mix. Flatten in pan, cook till crispy. XX
Heather Mills, English charity campaigner & former model

Paprika Potatoes @CountryLets
Boil new potatoes for 10 mins, put on baking tray & crush lightly. Drizzle w OO & sprinkle w paprika. S&P. Bake 20 mins.

Bubble & Squeak @helen_kara
Peel, boil & mash spuds. Slice & steam cabbage. Mix w lots of butter & S&P. Fry big spoonfuls in hot oil until brown.

Sweet Potato Wedges @CountryLets
In paper bag mix sweet potato chips, oil, S&P, cayenne pepper. Shake til coated. Baking tray 220c 20mins. Turn, cook 20mins more.

Herbed Potatoes @janjonesauthor
Fry masses finely-sliced onions & oregano in oil until caramelising. Add cooked new potatoes, gently move around hot pan until mixed.
Jan Jones, award-winning author of Regency romance & contemporary romantic comedy

Kenny's Patented Potato Cakes
@davekenny

Creamy mash, whipped w Parmesan & cheddar sauce. Fry in butter. For cheese sauce see page 71

Dave Kenny, *Sunday Tribune* columnist, author (*Erindipity, Erindipity Rides Again*), miscellanist, musician & occasional broadcaster

Best Mash *@helen_kara*
Slice leeks & fry in butter. Boil floury spuds til soft. Drain, mash w a little milk. Mix in leeks. Season, use to top shepherd's pie.

For Shepherd's Pie see page 98

@HobbyMaster
Tip: to make light fluffier mashed potatoes add a pinch of baking powder before whipping.

Sandwiches

Are you sick to death of ham and cheese, or peanut butter and jam? A sandwich is often the ideal option for a light meal, especially at lunchtime, but it's easy to get into a rut and eat the same thing over and over ... and over ... again. Well, check out this chapter for a host of fantastic sandwich ideas to shake up those boring old sarnies! You'll get some terrific inspiration for school lunchboxes here, too. Sandwiches aren't just for lunch, either. Take a look at the fantastic hot sandwiches later in the chapter – who says a sandwich can't be a full meal?

Simple Sandwiches

Amanda-Wich @Amanda_Holden
My favourite sandwich? Off the top of my head I would say cheese & Marmite sandwiches on Granary w a slice of cold cucumber! X
Amanda Holden, actress, television personality & judge on *Britain's Got Talent*.

V | **⏲**

The Sexiest Sandwich EVER
@cathryanhoward
Wholegrain bread, mayo, lettuce, crispy maple bacon & avocado. Warning: may cause avocado addiction.

L

TWEET TREATS 37

Peanut Butter & Banana Sandwich
@DazedPuckBunny
Cut crust off soft white bread, smear w peanut butter, honey & sliced banana. Serve w milk.

L

Double Butter Sandwich *@benshephard*
Two slices brown bread. Toast lightly. Once ready lather liberally w butter. Then dollop peanut butter on, spread & scoff!
Ben Shephard, television presenter with Sky Sports.

V L 🕐

Phil's Fave Filling *@Schofe*
Spread 2 slices bread generously w butter. Pile on garden peas – slightly minted if feeling adventurous! S&P. Voila! Enjoy your tasty snack.
Phillip Schofield, popular television personality.

L V

Mega Omega *@helen_kara*
Spread fresh brown bread w cream cheese. Chop avocadoes & smoked salmon, toss in lemon juice, sprinkle black pepper, pile on bread.

Low-Fat Wrap *@janetravers*
Spread a tortilla w tsp pesto, tsp low-fat mayonnaise. Add chicken/turkey, lettuce, whole basil leaves, cherry tomatoes, roll, scoff.

L

Classy Open Sandwich @MJulieMiller
Good bread, add dollop Italian chestnut honey, chunk of gorgonzola & a whole walnut.

V **L**

Pan-tumaca @SCallejo
Open french bread in half, rub fresh tomato on it, rub garlic, drizzle oil & spread serrano ham on top.

L

Egg Salad Sandwich @darrenshan
Boil an egg. Mix it w a dollop of salad cream. Get 2 slices of bread. Make a sandwich. That's as far as my culinary skills go!!
Darren Shan, author of freakily fantastical & demonically delightful books for children & adults.

Crunchy Open Sandwich @ukegnome
Put chicken, sweetcorn, celery, pineapple, OO, lemon juice & few pinches sugar in bowl. Combine. Pile on top of bread.

Toaster Required!

Toastie Tip @richclements
Can't cook but here's a tip - when making cheese on toast spread a layer of English mustard & melt cheese over it, yum!
Richmond Clements, Editor of Futurequake Press.

Best BLT @AllieDillon
Pick prime garden tomato & buttercrunch lettuce. Fry thick bacon. Toast homemade bread. Caress bread w mayo. Layer. S&P. Munch.

[L]

Salmon Spread Sandwich @austenonly
Small piece poached salmon, add mayo, lemon juice, black pepper, salt & whiz in blender. Spread on sliced toasted baguette.

[clock]

Chilli Tomato Ciabatta @MarkMoraghan
Ciabatta drizzled w EVOO, toasted chopped garlic, chilli, tomatoes, red onion, sesame seeds, small amount balsamic glaze.
Mark Moraghan, British actor & singer (*Peak Practice, Heartbeat, Brookside, Holby City*).

[L]

Pizza Bagel @clairecatrina
Toast bagel halves, spread w tomato purée. Sprinkle w cheese, anchovies on top. Add chopped tomatoes & halved olives. 180c 10mins.

[clock]

Cheat's Pizza @ClaireAllan
Red sauce, cheese, on bread toasted under the grill. Sounds vile, tastes divine. Basically a red sauce sambo aka cheap pizza!
Claire Allan, best-selling author of *Rainy Days & Tuesdays* among others.

[V] [L] [book]

Love-It-Or-Loathe-It Toastie
@LesleyPearse

Spread toast w butter & marmite. Thick slices of cheese on top & grill. Add tomato slices. Yum.

Lesley Pearse, prolific novelist of 18 books including *Never Look Back*, *Trust Me* & latest *Belle*.

V

Quesadilla Sandwich *@cathyby*

Tortilla in hot pan, layer meltable cheese (jarlsberg) & thin cured ham, another tortilla on top. Brown both sides in pan, serve w salsa.

L

Italian Sandwich *@charliedncn*

Slice ciabatta, toast lightly & rub w roasted garlic. Top w buffalo mozzarella, tomato, fresh basil & twist of black pepper. Enjoy!

Terrific Toastie *@christinemosler*

Grill bread one side. Mix chopped onion, chilli powder, mustard, grated cheddar. Spread on ungrilled side. Grill it. Eat.

Tuna Toastie *@hmhunt*

Mash tin of tuna & add chopped olives & mayonnaise to taste. Spread on hot buttered toast.

L 🕒

TWEET TREATS

Instant Croque Monsieur @jenoconnell
Toast 1 side of bread. Grated swiss, drizzle cream, smidge mustard. Mix, spread on other side bread, grill.
Jennifer O'Connell, founding editor of *TheJournal.ie*, columnist with *Sunday Business Post*, occasional broadcaster.

V

Chilli Beans on Toast @Shobnagulati
Fry ½ onion, 1tsp ginger, green chilli chopped, ½tsp cumin, pinch coriander. Add can baked beans, serve on toasted granary bread.
Actress Shobna Gulati, best known for her role as Sunita on *Coronation Street*.

V

@Shobnagulati
Tip: Be careful w the chilli, de-seed first & mind your eyes!!!
Actress Shobna Gulati, best known for her role as Sunita on *Coronation Street*.

💡

Mushrooms On Toast @christinemosler
Fry mushrooms in butter, garlic, pepper. Grill toast one side, grate cheese onto other side, top w mushrooms, grill until bubbly.

Open Ranch Sandwich @DazedPuckBunny
Cube roast turkey, stir in bowl w mayo, 3tbsp Ranch dressing, diced celery. Serve on warm toast.

L

Avocado Sandwich @paulakahumbu
Avocado slices, slices cheddar cheese, tomato, squeeze lemon juice, S&P between buttered toast. Heaven!
Paula Kahumbu, ecologist, conservationist & children's author.

V

What I Call 'A Toasted Sandwich' @mermhart
Toast bread. Microwave cheese to melt. Cheese on toast. Worcestershire sauce. Layer of ham. Mustard. Another layer cheese. Yum.
Miranda Hart, comedy actress & writer known for *Hyperdrive, Absolutely Fabulous, Comic Relief does Fame Academy* & her own sitcom *Miranda*.

L

Chilli Toast @jacr13
Take a slice of toast, top w peanut butter (crunchy or smooth) & as many jalapenos as you can handle. Surprisingly good!

L

Sweet'N'Salt @LadyLittleton
Grill rashers. Split fruit buns & toast each half, place grilled bacon between halves. Salty bacon, sweet warm fruit bread. Eat & enjoy!

Best Sandwich Ever @literaticat
Pastrami & swiss toasted on sourdough baguette w jalapeno & avocado. NOM!

TWEET TREATS 43

Double-Decker Special @mdemuffywriter
L — Toast 3 slices wholemeal bread. Layer – bread, mayo, lettuce, cheese, crispy bacon, bread, mayo, lettuce, cheese, boiled egg, mayo, bread.

Lazy Snack @clairehennessy
★ — Pitta bread at ¾ usual toasting strength, fill w cheese & crisps, return to toaster for 30 secs.
Prolific author of *Dear Diary* & eight other books for teens.

Easy Open Toastie @mikelcu
V — Avocado on toast topped w Shropshire Blue is to die for!

Chicken Toastie @mduffywriter
L — Mix chopped cooked chicken breast, chopped tomato & grated cheese. Add 1tbsp pesto. Spread over french bread. Grill till bubbly.

Sweet Treat Toastie @mrsredboots
V — Toast bread. Spread w peanut butter. Top w bananas sliced lengthways. Sprinkle brown sugar & grill until sugar bubbles.

Pizza Turnover @PenguinGalaxy
V — 2 mini naans in sarnie toaster, put in cheese, spring onion, red pepper, tomato purée & anything else for pizza turnover!

Cheese Lovers' Dream @PositivelyBeaut
Spread half ciabatta bread w mascarpone cheese, sprinkle w blue cheese & chopped walnuts, bake in warm oven until melted.

Reuben Sandwich @the0phrastus
Rye bread, Thousand Island dressing, sauerkraut, butter, swiss cheese, pastrami – toast buttered bread in frying pan, assemble, eat.
Chris Howard, fantasy & science fiction author (*Saltwater Witch, Seaborn*) & illustrator.

Super Sandwiches to Make a Meal of!

Fruity Toasted Treat @ClodaghMMurphy
Mix cream cheese, grated Cheddar, grated apple, Tabasco, S&P. Make wholemeal bread sandwich. Fry in butter both sides.
Author of *The Disengagement Ring* & *Girl in a Spin*

Smoked Salmon Sandwich @CountryLets
Slice baguette thinly, little OO, bake till crisp. Top w cream cheese & smoked salmon, squeeze of lemon & black pepper.

Summer in a Sandwich @DazedPuckBunny
Spread french bread w OO, toast in pan, top w slice of creamy havarti & sliced strawberries, serve warm.

[L]

Luxury Toastie @DazedPuckBunny
Smear bread w fig spread, couple slices of brie, couple slices of apple, second slice bread on top, butter outsides, toast on skillet.

Good Enough for Guests @goodtoweet
Sauté wild mushrooms crushed garlic & S&P in butter, add dash cream. Serve on griddled sourdough, garnish w chopped chervil/parsley.

Protein-Packed Pitta @ZoeTyler
Chop garlic, onion, mange tout, bell pepper, mushrooms. Fry. Add tuna & lemon juice. Lace hot pitta w hummus. Fill.

Zoe Tyler, vocal trainer, singer, & judge on *How Do You Solve a Problem Like Maria*, *Hairspray: The School Musical* and others.

Spear Sandwich @helen_kara
Toss asparagus stalks in OO & sea salt. Roast. Garnish w Parmesan curls & serve on freshly-baked baguette.

[L]

Baked Bean Fold-Over @helen_kara
[V] Per person: 2 Staffordshire oatcakes, ½ tin baked beans, 56g grated cheese. Cover ½ each oatcake w beans & cheese, fold, heat thru.

@janetravers
Staffordshire oatcakes are like oatmeal pancakes – alternatively, you could use wholemeal pancakes in the above recipe.

Steak Sandwich @hmhinkle
[L] Cut steak into strips, pan fry. Add to roll or bread of choice. Top w sautéed onions & peppers, mayo & mozzarella cheese.

Lobster Roll @HOHWwriter
Pick apart meat of 1 lobster, mix w mayo, chopped celery, S&P. Serve on buttered, toasted bun. [L]

Creamy Mushroom Toast @Mrs_Moons
[V] Fry mushrooms in butter, garlic, pepper. Splash of cream, drizzle w balsamic vinegar, lots parsley. Serve on toasted ciabatta.

Tuna Melt @NettieWriter
Open a panini, fill w tuna & mayo, sprinkle w cheddar or double Gloucester, close & grill until golden. [L]

Philly Cheese Steak Sandwich *@NettieWriter*
Soften onion & mushrooms in oil, add shredded minute-steak. When cooked add provolone cheese. Once melted pile onto long roll.

Smoked Tofu Sandwich *@sgwarnog*
Slice smoked tofu & marinate in soy sauce. Fry in hot oil. Sandwich in toasted bread w mustard.

Mighty Meat-Free *@squeakattack*
Spray portobello mushrooms w oil, grill. Grilled goats cheese on top, drizzle w pesto. Put on nice bread or bun, add rocket. Nommy!

Hot Chicken Baguette *@MrUku*
Chop & fry chicken breast, mushrooms, onion & peppers w a little Cajun spice. Serve in a baguette lined w mayo & lettuce.

Salads & Dressings

Salads are endlessly versatile; they can be side dishes, starters or full meals. Although only popularised for modern palates in the US in the late nineteenth century, records show that the Romans ate dishes of mixed greens with a dressing, and the Babylonians were known to have used a dressing of oil and vinegar on greens two thousand years ago.

For many people 'salad' is a bad word, conjuring images of limp lettuce leaves and soggy tomato, but the reality can be vastly different; you can use salad vegetables, pulses, grains and fruits in endless combinations. If you're tired of the same basic green salad, you'll find plenty of inspiration on the following pages to change up your menu. The array of dressings alone will enliven any salad, no matter how basic.

Unless otherwise stated in any of the following recipes, remember that the standard ratio for oil-based dressings is three parts oil to one part acid (lemon juice or vinegar).

Side Salads

Sweet'n'Spicy Salad @joannechocolat
Avocado. Mango. Slice. Mix. Add sticky balsamic, bit of fresh chilli. Basil leaves. Terrific salad – goes well w margaritas.
Joanne Harris, multi-award winning & best-selling author of *Chocolat*, judge of the Whitbread & Orange prizes.

TWEET TREATS 49

Fruity Feta Salad @CafeFresh
Watermelon, feta, cherry tomato, thinly-sliced red onion & a drizzle of EVOO – maybe a hint of mint!

Summer Salmon Salad @CountryLets
Strips of cucumber w strips of smoked salmon on a plate. Mix horseradish, Greek yogurt, crème fraîche, lemon, S&P, pour over.

Rainbow Coleslaw @gardenfix
Grate carrots, red cabbage, add small can drained crushed pineapple, leftover dill pickle juice, combine.

Mighty Mung @HazelKLarkin
Tip a tin of mung beans into a bowl, stir in 3tbsp desiccated coconut, 2tbsp tamari, ½ tsp garam masala & pinch chilli flakes.

Zesty Avocado Salad @helen_kara
Segment pink grapefruit & remove all pith. Slice avocado. Arrange on plate(s), drizzle OO & balsamic vinegar, sprinkle salt.

Wilted Radicchio Salad @hi5living
Drizzle radicchio (chicory) leaves w OO, sprinkle w parmesan. Grill in oven until leaves soften. Sprinkle w balsamic vinegar.

Tropical Rice Salad @hmhunt
To cold leftover rice add tinned/fresh pineapple chunks, mandarins cut small, desiccated coconut & sultanas.

Bean Salad @JackyHSF
Mix 225g each pinto, black, garbanzo & kidney beans. Add 1 chopped red onion, bunch chopped coriander. Stir in 120ml rice vinegar. Season.

Curried Rice Salad @janetravers
Dressing: mayonnaise & curry powder to taste. Combine w cold boiled rice, raisins & chopped apple.

Cabbage Salad @paulakahumbu
Thinly slice 240g cold hard cabbage, add juice 1 lemon, 1tbsp EVOO, salt. Eat immediately.
Paula Kahumbu, ecologist, conservationist & children's author.

Left-over Rice Salad @juxtabook
Add peas, finely-chopped celery, chopped walnuts, grated ginger, garlic, dress w sesame oil & sherry.

TWEET TREATS 51

Easy Pasta Salad @janetravers
Cook pasta bows, cool under cold tap. Add unroasted peanuts. Dressing: natural yogurt w splash orange juice, mix all together.

Beetroot Slaw @LevParikian
Grate equal quantities of raw beetroot & carrot. Enrich mayonnaise w some OO & mustard. S&P, obviously. Mix.

Broccoli Salad @mduffywriter
Chop head broccoli, discarding stalks. Cubes feta cheese, cherry tomatoes, peanuts. Mayonnaise & squeeze lemon.

Amazing Avocado salad @paulakahumbu
Finely chop 2 cloves garlic w salt & the juice of 1 lemon. Add to coarsely-chopped avocado & chill for 3 hrs.
Paula Kahumbu, ecologist, conservationist & children's author.

Couscous Salad @mduffywriter
Cover 170g couscous in boiling water 10mins. Stir in chopped onion, sundried tomatoes, cucumber, coriander, tbsp OO, lemon juice.

Mixed Bean Salad @PenguinGalaxy
1 tin mixed beans, balsamic vinegar, OO, parsley, cucumber, red pepper, spring onion, all finely chopped.

Pipirana (A Spanish recipe, translates as 'toad pee'!) @PenguinGalaxy
Very finely-chopped tomato, peppers, cucumber, garlic. Lots of salt, vinegar & OO.

Summer Salad @mollydcampbell
To cottage cheese, add finely-chopped chives, carrot, radish, celery, & parsley.

Cool As A ... @SarahTregear
Peel & slice cucumber, wipe w kitchen roll. Place in bowl, sprinkle w 2tbsp caster sugar, 2tbsp white wine vinegar, fresh mint.

Austrian Potato Salad @acediscovery
Boil & slice potatoes, chop red/spring onions, crush garlic, chop chives. Mix w oil, water & vinegar.

Best Potato Salad @Chiddle84
Hardboil 2 eggs, leave to cool. Boil enough potatoes for 2 people, mash w spring onion, lashings of milk, butter, S&P, cut in egg. Mix.

Main Course Salads

Salmagundi @julianstockwin
18th-century 'composed salad' – cured fish, cold meat, lettuce, egg, herbs, nasturtium flowers. Yum!
Julian Stockwin, best-selling author of the historical *Thomas Kydd* series.

[L]

Tuna Salad @40again
Shredded rocket & lettuce, halved cherry tomatoes, chunks cucumber, red onion. Top w flaked, drained tuna, drizzle w lemon oil, chill.

Brown Rice Salad @Buckswriter
Cook brown rice, add vinaigrette when still warm. Cool, add sultanas, nuts, spring onions, cucumber, tomatoes, pepper & apple.

[L] [♥]

Rocket Feta Pepper Salad @BuddingGourmet
Fresh rocket (arugula), red & yellow peppers, cubed feta, fresh lime, sea salt & a touch of balsamic vinegar.

Moroccan Couscous Salad @CafeFresh
Add diced peppers, courgette, cherry tomatoes, cucumber, freshly-chopped mint & parsley to couscous. Dressing of lemon, garlic & OO.

[V] [♥]

Luxury Mango Salad @paulakahumbu
Pile steamed snow peas & sliced mango on bed of lettuce, cress & rocket. Top w crumbled feta, chopped walnuts & raspberry dressing.
Paula Kahumbu, ecologist, conservationist & children's author.

L ♥

Easter Parade Salad @Chiddle84
Dressing: cumin, lemon juice, OO. Rub bowl w garlic. Mix coriander, salad leaves, thin sliced onion, petits pois, HB egg. Sprinkle Parmesan.

Lentil Potato Salad @christinemosler
Cook puy lentils, new potatoes & green beans. Mix w sliced red onions, red peppers tomatoes, olives, basil & balsamic vinegar. S&P.

♥

Tuna Nicoise @CountryLets
To salad leaves add tuna, cooked sliced potatoes, green beans, anchovies, black olives. Mix & dress w vinaigrette, top w boiled egg.

♥

Greek Salad @CountryLets
Slice red onion, tomatoes, olives, green pepper. Dress w red wine vinegar, S&P, OO. Top w feta.

♥ L

TWEET TREATS

Heavenly Halloumi @CountryLets
Mix strawberries w balsamic vinegar, EVOO, S&P. Fry slices of halloumi, serve w rocket, basil, mint leaves, Parma ham & strawberries.

Sweet Fig Salad @CountryLets
Roast figs w honey. Serve w Parma ham, buffalo mozzarella, salad leaves & basil. Dress w lemon, EVOO, S&P.

Pasta Salad @mduffywriter
Cook pasta ribbons & cool. Blanch bunch fresh spinach & stir into pasta. Dry fry pine nuts & sunflower seeds, add. Mayonnaise.

Protein-Packed Salad @MJulieMiller
Mix 2 tins cannellini, tuna, lemon zest & juice, pitted green olives, diced red pepper, paper-thin sliced garlic. Serve w good bread.

Real Man's Pasta Salad @PenguinGalaxy
Fry spring onions, peppers, bacon & mushrooms. Add parsley, honey, mustard, mayo, yogurt. Cool, add to pasta, serve on bed of lettuce.

Mango & Lobster Salad @tcordrey
Slice mango into strips. Slice (cooked) lobster flesh. Keep claws whole. Toss all w salad leaves & French dressing.

Divine Dressings
Oil & Vinegar-Based Dressings

Awesomeness Salad Dressing @JasonBradbury
Coaster-sized dollop EVOO (first press). Thick, aged balsamic vinegar. Ground black pepper. Sea salt. Demerara sugar. Combine.

Jason Bradbury, *The Gadget Show* host & children's author.

Honey Mustard Vinaigrette @bleuviolettes
Mix: 2 parts OO, 1 part balsamic vinegar, 1 part wholegrain mustard, 1 part honey. Excellent as dressing, dip, or marinade.

Dynamite Dressing @helen_kara
Crushed fresh garlic, EVOO, fresh lemon juice, paprika, chilli powder, salt, mix to taste.

Thick Any-Jam Vinaigrette @honeysock
2 parts jam, 2 parts OO, 1 part vinegar, grind of pepper, few drops of vanilla essence. Shake well to combine.

Chilli-Garlic Salad Dressing @jacr13
60ml OO, 1tsp extra hot chilli powder, 1 clove garlic, crushed. Adjust amounts for taste/quantity needed.

Carrot Miso Salad Dressing @JudyJooIronChef
60ml corn oil, 60ml rice vinegar, 3tbsp miso soup, 1tbsp roasted sesame oil, 2 cooked carrots, 1tbsp lime juice, S&P. Blend.
Judy Joo, chef, food writer & judge on *Iron Chef UK*.

French Dressing @RebeccaEmin
1tsp mustard, 1tsp sugar, 2tbsp vinegar & 4tbsp OO in a jar. Shake & serve.

Creamy Dressings

Low-cal Salad Dressing @gardenfix
Yogurt, thinned w milk, w crushed garlic, fresh dill, salt. Use on baby spinach soon.

Mayonnaise @goodtoweet
By hand, beat 2 egg yolks w ½tsp Dijon mustard, 1 dsp white wine vinegar. Beat in 225ml sunflower oil SLOWLY, drop by drop. S&P.

Coleslaw Dressing @helen_kara
Half mayonnaise, half plain yogurt, mix well, season w salt, pepper & fresh lemon juice to taste.

Tarragon Salad Dressing @lucywaverman
Whisk 1tsp chopped tarragon, 2tsp mayo, 1tsp Dijon mustard, 2tsp chopped shallots, 2tsp white wine vinegar, 50ml OO, S&P.
Lucy Waverman, one of Canada's favourite culinary personalities: editor, columnist & teacher.

Creamy Garlic Dressing @JackyHSF
Whisk 2 parts sour cream, 1 part each mayo & milk, 1tsp garlic, pinch cayenne. Dress lettuce, sliced onion, can mandarins, sliced mushrooms.

Creamy Salad Dressing @PenguinGalaxy
Grated parmesan, mint sauce & yogurt. Mint sauce best if made w fresh leaves. Great w lettuce!

Soups & Sauces

There aren't many foods that strike fear into my heart when I come to prepare them, but for some reason soup always has. Having been told for years how incredibly easy and foolproof soup was, I was utterly disheartened at my first few efforts, which all turned into tasteless, watery mush.

Gathering these recipes for *Tweet Treats*, however, gave me renewed interest in the versatility of soup, and taught me that the greatest mistake I was making was simply over-egging the pudding (if you'll pardon the mixed metaphor!). The simplicity and variety of recipes on the following pages will inspire even the most soup-phobic among you, especially when you see what you can do with five minutes and a microwave.

The wonderful thing about soup is that you don't need to be too precise about weights and measures. Just throw everything in the pot and add as much or as little stock as you think you need. It brings creativity back to cooking, even though it's so simple.

Soups make terrific starters, but to really finish off a meal beautifully you sometimes need a sauce. On the following pages you'll find simple ideas to perk up fish, liven up chicken and pad out pasta – and not a complicated roux in sight!

Soups Lighter Soups

Broccoli Soup @parmindernagra
Steam broccoli, keep water, slowly blitz broccoli, adding the water to desired thickness, season & serve! xx :)

Parminder Nagra, English actress best known for her roles in *Bend it like Beckham* & as Neela in *ER*.

Roast Tomato Soup @Bridget_CooKs
Slice 20 toms in ½, sprinkle w brown sugar, cumin, sea salt, black pepper, EVOO. Roast oven 200c 45mins. Purée all. Season & serve.

Consommé @CelizMurray
Reduce & strain vegetable stock, add in organic bouillon, simmer. Serve w wholemeal bread, lightly buttered.

Sweet Squash Soup @Colmogorman
Roast diced squash, quartered apples & onion plus garlic & a red chilli. Blend w stock & serve w coriander pesto. For coriander pesto see page 68

Colm O'Gorman, author of *Beyond Belief*, activist, director of Amnesty International Ireland, founder of One in Four

French Onion Soup @chiddle84
Heat 2tbsp oil,56g buttr,700g onion,2clv garlic,½tsp sugar.Cook 6mins,reduce heat 30mins.Add1L beefstock,275ml wh.wine.Cook 1hr.2tbsp cognac

@helen_kara
Tip: If making a dark savoury soup or stew, increase complexity of flavour by adding a tablespoon of 100% cocoa. Nobody will guess.

Easy Leftover Soup @chadwickauthor
Leftover peppers, tomatoes, onions. Roast 180c in splash of oil & cup of water 25 mins. Blitz. Add extra liquid & season.

Elizabeth Chadwick, award-winning, best-selling author of historical fiction including *To Defy a King* & *Lady of the English*.

Low Fat Soup @christinemosler
Peel butternut squash, chop into large chunks. Roast 180c 30mins w a little OO. Whizz w bouillon stock, parsley, pepper. Serve.

Lentil Tomato Soup @dorristheloris
Onion, carrot, celery, garlic: fry in OO. Add green lentils, tin tomatoes, herbs, stock, 120ml OO. Yummy Soup!

Butternut Soup @gardenfix
Sautéed onions (lots), butternut squash cubes, barely cover w chicken stock. Simmer till tender. Season w sage. Purée.

Nettle Soup @goodtoweet
Chop 1 onion&1 potato.Sweat in 3tbsp butter till soft.Add 1L chicken stock.When veg soft add handful of nettles. Simmer 2 mins. Blitz.

[L]

Easy Vegetable Soup @SarahBrownUK
Add chopped leek, carrot, potato to homemade chicken or veg stock, heat for 20 mins & season, yum.
Sarah Brown, mother & charity campaigner, married to former Prime Minister Gordon Brown.

[L] [⏲] [📚]

Rasam @HazelKLarkin
Mash 10 cloves of garlic & fry. Add 1tsp cumin, coriander, 2 tins tomatoes, splash of water. South Indian soup, Good for colds.

[♥] [L]

Root Soup @helen_kara
Fry onion, garlic. Add chunks of mixed root veg & enough stock to cover. Simmer till veg soft, blend w a little milk, season.

[V] [L]

@helen_kara
Tip: for any blended vegetable soup (mushroom, tomato, carrot etc) roast the veggies first for a more intense flavour.

Personal Pea Soup @hprw
Cook mugful frozen peas in mugful milk till done; add pinch dried chillies; liquidise smooth. Pea soup for one!

Lazy Version Of Jewish Chicken Soup @sarramanning
1 pkt Osem Chicken noodle soup, leftover roast chicken & juices, chicken stock cube, 1½L boiling water. Simmer 15 mins. Cures all ills.

Sarra Manning, popular author for adults (*Unsticky* and *You Don't Have to Say You Love Me*) & teens (*The Diary of a Crush* trilogy & others).

Ginger Lentil Soup @MrsTrevithick
(Per person) 200g red lentils, 1 diced carrot, pinch powdered ginger. Sweat in butter. Add water/orange juice to taste, simmer till soft. Yum.

Celery Soup @RosalindAdam
Fry 2 onions in butter, add 8 sliced celery sticks, 1 carrot, 3 bay leaves, stock & seasoning. Simmer, remove bay. Blitz.

@helen_kara
Tip: To increase protein content of any blended veggie soup, add a pack of silken tofu before blending. Won't affect flavour.

Spiced Lentil Soup @MrsTrevithick
(Per person) 1 cup red lentils, pinch each turmeric, cumin. Sweat in oil. Add 1tsp tomato purée, water. Simmer2soft, flaked almonds, eat.

Salmorejo @SCallejo
Liquidise 1kg tomatoes, 1 garlic, large piece dry bread, 20ml balsamic vinegar. W motor running add 250ml OO.

@SCallejo
Tip: Salmorejo should be thick & some put boiled egg on it, poached egg (if you can make it) or otherwise even bits of apple.

Red Roast Soup @TheWriteRach
Dice:1 but'nut squash,2sweet potatoes,2red onions,2 red peppers.Drizzle OO.Roast 1hr.Blend w enough veg stock to right thickness. S&P.

Hearty Soups

Leek & Potato Soup @chadwickauthor
Chop 4 large leeks, 2 potatoes, 1 onion, 30g smoked bacon. Sauté in butter, add 500ml chicken stock (more if needed). Simmer & blitz.

Elizabeth Chadwick, award-winning, best-selling author of historical fiction, including *To Defy a King* & *Lady of the English*

North-East Clam Chowder @AllieDillon
[L] Fry bacon, then celery & onions in bacon tears. Add in clam juice, diced potatoes, bay leaves. Simmer. Add clams, corn, milk, butter.

Potato Soup @goodtoweet
[V] Chop 1 onion & 3 spuds, sweat in butter. Add 600ml stock, 3tsp fresh thyme leaves, S&P. Simmer 20 min. Dash of cream. Blitz. [L]

Cream Of Tomato Soup @christinemosler
[V] Heat 250ml passata. Stir in 600ml half milk, half cream mixed. Bring to boil, simmer 5 mins. Add pinch sugar. [L] [🕐]

Ham & Pea Soup @dorristheloris
[L] In saucepan: ham, soaked brothmix or split peas, onion, leek, carrot, potato, ham stock, bay leaf. Boil, simmer 1-2 hrs till yum!

Hearty Beet Soup @JackyHSF
[L] Large pan, cover 1.8kg peeled beets w water. 2 diced potatoes, 5 chopped onions. Boil. Simmer 1hr. 60ml lem juic. Add 4 beaten eggs slow, stirring.

Butternut Squash Soup @mattjesson
Halve b'nut squash, butter, roast 30min. Onion & garlic, fry. Scoop flesh to pan, just cover w stock. Simmer 5min, 50ml cream, herbs. Whiz.

Parsnip & Apple Soup @MrsTrevithick
Chopped 75% parsnip 25% Bramley, good pinch cinnamon, sweat in butter, add water. Simmer until soft, pulverise, serve, mmmm....

Warming Pumpkin Soup @PositivelyBeaut
500ml vegetable stock, 500g roast pumpkin, 2 chopped leeks, salt, 1tbsp butter. Simmer 20 mins. Whiz, add tbsp cream, sprinkle nutmeg.

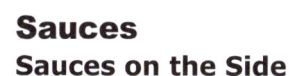

Sauces
Sauces on the Side

Gremolata @antonycotton
Grate the peel of 1 lemon, add a handful of chopped flat-leaf parsley & 2tsp capers. Spoon over fillet steak.

Antony Cotton, actor best known for his role as Sean in *Coronation Street*

Great Garlic Sauce @helen_kara
Gently fry shallots, garlic, parsley. Slosh white wine, reduce, add créme fraîche, S&P. Good w meat, fish or pasta.

Basil Cream @honeysock
240ml heavy cream, handful fresh-chopped basil, pinch salt. Boil until thick. Best drizzled on grilled beef fillet medallions.

Mrs Fry's Saucy Surprise @MrsStephenFry
Smear lovingly & beat feverishly until fully hardened. Whip to a frenzy then drizzle before taking a cold shower & preparing your meal.
'Edna Fry', Stephen Fry's downtrodden 'wife' & author of *Mrs Fry's Diary*.

Citrus Parsley Paste @goodtoweet
Crush 1 garlic clove, juice ½ lemon, 200g black olives, 1tbsp parsley, 3tbsp EVOO, S&P to make rough paste. Serve w pink lamb or mackerel.

Dill Sauce @rebeccaebrown
250ml milk. Mix some w 1tbsp cornflour, then add rest of milk & heat w butter. Add dill & 2 drops lemon oil. Nice sauce for fish.

Coriander Pesto @Colmogorman
Whizz 50g coriander, 1tbsp walnuts, 1tsp chilli flakes, 1tbsp lemon juice, 8tbsp OO & Parmesan to taste. Hey Pesto!
Colm O'Gorman, author of *Beyond Belief*, activist, director of Amnesty International Ireland, founder of One in Four.

Spinach Pesto *@mduffywriter*
Whizz handful spinach, fresh basil, 30g Parmesan, clove garlic in blender. Add few drops lemon juice & OO till paste. Fridge.

Chilli Pesto *@coradevine*
Basil, parsley, pine nuts, Parmesan, fresh garlic, crushed chilli, OO, lemon juice, salt; blend!

Mayonnaise *@goodtoweet*
By hand, beat 2 egg yolks w ½tsp Dijon, 1dsp white wine vinegar. Beat in 225ml sunflower oil SLOWLY, drop by drop. S&P.

Tartar Sauce *@goodtoweet*
Mix lots of finely-chopped chives, gherkins, capers into good mayonnaise. Season & spike w a squeeze of lemon juice.

Mild Pico De Gallo Sauce *@DazedPuckBunny*
Dice tomatoes w 2tbsp coriander leaves, minced red onion, 1tbsp lime juice & a pinch of garlic.

TWEET TREATS

Fancy Ketchup @Harlequin229
240ml ketchup, 1tbsp Worcestershire sauce, 1tbsp soy sauce, 1tbsp smoked paprika, 1tbsp garlic. Mix, serve. Goes well w steak.

Sauces That Make a Meal

Great Chilli Sauce @paulakahumbu
Char 300g chillis. Fry 5 cloves garlic. Add 100g chopped fresh coriander, 1tsp salt, 240ml vinegar. Boil 5 mins.
Paula Kahumbu, ecologist, conservationist & children's author.

Sweet & Sour Sauce @NettieWriter
6dsp sugar, 2dsp cornflour, 2dsp soysauce, 8dsp vinegar, 2dsp tomato purée, salt, 380ml water. In pan, mix, bring to slow boil stirring.

Sticky Duck Glaze @Caro_lann
Shred some ginger finely. Add juice of 4 lemons & 2tbsp honey. Mix & pour over duck breast. Bake until skin blackened.

Tikka Sauce @NettieWriter
Marinate chicken in fat free yogurt w 3tbsp OO, 1tbsp lemon juice, 4tbsp tikka spices. Grill.

Masala Sauce @NettieWriter
Sweat some onion, add can chopped tomatoes, little passata, 2tbsp tikka spices, simmer. Add cream, warm thru.

Cheese Sauce @jennyfoxe
40g butter, 40g flour, 570ml milk in a pan. Stir to melt & combine, bring to boil. Reduce heat, simmer 5 mins. 100g cheese, stir to melt.

Blue Cheese Sauce @helen_kara
Fry red onion w garlic until soft. Stir in ½ soft blue cheese & ½ crème fraîche, season to taste. Great w gnocchi.

@janetravers
Tip: Make amazing cheese sauce by stirring in 1tsp of English mustard when cooked.

Veggie Gravy @helen_kara
Fry onion & mushroom with fresh thyme till brown. Add flour, red wine, veg stock slowly, then Marmite, tamari, tomato purée.

TWEET TREATS

Fish

Fish is healthy, versatile and makes a terrific family meal – and yet very few of us eat as much of it as we should. It looks fiddly and we often let ourselves be put off by scales, heads and eyes and the thoughts of messy preparation.

No more! With the easy recipes on the following pages, there are no excuses for not serving fish. If you're squeamish, there are plenty of recipes that feature pre-prepared – or even pre-cooked – fish; if you're tight on time, some of these recipes literally could not be quicker (five minutes in a microwave rivals even the fastest ready-meal). There are recipes here for every eventuality – meals that kids will love, crowd-pleasers, even meals to impress a group of friends. Head for your local fishmongers then get stuck in!

Easy Recipes With Pre-Cooked Fish

Friday Night Light Meal @buzzbissinger
Open can tuna,drain.Add mayo,hot curry pwdr,red pepper.Mix as thoroughly as poss under circumstances. Eat from can.Feel strangely unsatisfied
Harry Gerard Bissinger III, known as Buzz Bissinger, Author of *Friday Night Lights, Prayer for City, 3 Nights in August*. Contributing editor *Vanity Fair*.

Smoked Salmon Pasta @beckyl_j
Packet fresh pasta – cook as per instructions, drain. Mix in 1 tub crème fraîche, 1 packet smoked salmon trimmings, dill, lemon.

Easy Tuna Pilaf @RebeccaEmin
Cook some white rice. Add sweetcorn, tuna chunks, black olives, chopped tomatoes. Drizzle w balsamic vinegar & OO.

Fish Taco @charleebrawn
Iceberg lettuce, diced chopped tomatoes, grilled white tuna, mayo mixed w Sriracha spicy sauce, taco shell... put all this together!

Hot Potato Salad With Salmon @CountryLets
Boil new potatoes. Mix 2tbsp horseradish, juice 1 lemon, 2tbsp crème fraîche, black pepper. Stir into potatoes, add smoked salmon, serve.

Trout With Melon & Herb Salsa @tepilo
Mix peppercorns, spring onions, lime juice, caster sugar. Serve over cantaloupe melon & flaked smoked trout.
Property guru Sarah Beeny's website giving you an alternative way to buy/sell/let a home

TWEET TREATS 73

Fish Cakes @CountryLets
Add tin tuna, spring onion & flat-leaf parsley to leftover mash. Shape to form cakes, dip in egg then breadcrumbs. Fry.

L

Anchovy Linguine @goodtoweet
Add anchovy fillets, capers, ground dried chilli to your basic tomato pasta sauce. Serve w linguine. Sprinkle w breadcrumbs fried in EVOO.

Student Special @helen_kara
1 can condensed mushroom soup, 1 can tuna in brine, 500g frozen peas. Mix, heat, serve on pasta. Old student standby.

L

Easy Tuna Pasta @hmhunt
Cook pasta & drain, add tin of tuna & tin of sweetcorn. Stir in a knob of butter & sprinkle salt & ground black pepper.

L

Crunchy Tuna Bake @iknowhim
Tuna in thick-grain mustard cheese sauce. Add layer baked beans. Add layer creamy buttery mash. Top w crushed crisps. 180c 20mins.

For cheese sauce see page 71

Tuna & Tomato Bake @rebeccaebrown
Cooked pasta, tin tomatoes, 2 cans tuna. Mix in grated cheese & sprinkle more on top. Oven, high heat, 20 mins.

Tuna Fishcakes @janetravers
Drain can of tuna, mix w leftover mash, 1 egg, leftover veg e.g. cabbage. Form cakes, roll in breadcrumbs, fry.

Fishy Baked Potatoes @janetravers
Bake large potatoes, halve & scoop out. Mix potato w can drained tuna, can drained corn, crème fraîche if you have it. Refill skins, grill.

Cheese & Crab Dip @laurenfaith
220g lump crab meat, 220g cream cheese, dash Worcestershire, 1tbsp horseradish. Microwave 3min, sprinkle Old Bay spices. Serve w crudités.

Protein-Packed Pile On @MJulieMiller
Mix 2 tins cannellini, tuna, lemon zest & juice, pitted green olives, diced red pepper, paper-thin sliced garlic. Serve w good bread.

TWEET TREATS 75

No-Fuss Fish Dishes
Shellfish

⭐ Moroccan Shrimp @BettyBuckley
Sauté chopped garlic & onion, wok in OO.Add chopped veg & almonds then fresh shrimp. Add spices:masala, cumin, pepper, lem juice – mmm good!

Betty Buckley, American theatre, film & television actress & singer, known as the Voice of Broadway for her rendition of 'Memories' in *Cats*.

L

King Of The Sea @agnieszkasshoes
Marinate king prawns in soy, honey, ginger, allspice, chilli. Grill. Serve w samphire which has been cooked 3 mins in butter.

♥

⭐ Prawn Tempura @Bookwalter
Mix 240g flour, 120g cornflour, pour in chilled soda water until gloopy. Dip prawns, deep fry. Serve w lemon wedges.

Richard Jay Parker, author of acclaimed debut thriller *Stop Me*, shortlisted for CWA Dagger Award.

L

Moules Marinière @goodtoweet
Sweat 1 clove garlic, 1shallot in butter.Add 1kg mussels, 50ml white wine.Increase heat, cover.Cook til mussels open.Serve w juices&parsley.

Variation on Moules Marinière – Mussels With Paprika @CiaranMcNulty

Sweat leek & 2 cloves garlic, 1tsp paprika. Add glass white wine & 1kg mussels. Lid on for 7min. Add cream, parsley, squeeze lemon, serve.

L

Chilli Prawns @davidgilray

3tbsp OO & chopped chilli in a very hot pan. Add 300g peeled prawns & 4 cloves sliced garlic. 2 mins. Serve in bowls w bread.

L

Prawn Curry @GinGoddess

Fry onion, 1tsp garlic pickle in oil. Add tin toms, cook 15 mins. Add mushrooms cook5 mins. Add prawns, cook till hot through. Serve w rice.

Prawns In Garlic @humphreycushion

Soften lots of chopped garlic in 3 glugs of OO & knob of butter. Add 3 handfuls of large, juicy peeled prawns & sizzle.

L

Thai Prawn Curry @jadamthwaite

Stirfry garlic,ginger,lime leaves,lemongrass,chilli, basil,12-14 large raw prawns.Add 1can coconut milk, dash fish sauce,sugar.Simmer.Heaven.

Scallops In Garlic @tcordrey
Melt garlic butter in pan. Add scallops & fry 30 secs each side. Remove from heat. Squeeze over lemon & sprinkle a little salt.

Salmon

Salmon With Pesto @TrishWylie
Take 2 salmon fillets, smear w pesto, place in foil w 2tsp water & a squeeze of lemon juice. Bake 180c 10 mins approx.
Trish Wylie, award-winning Irish romance writer.

@janetravers
You can be certain that fish is fully cooked when it is completely opaque & flakes easily when pulled w a fork.

Salmon With Celeriac @bluepootle
Grill salmon. Roast celeriac, pancetta, red onion in spoonful of chicken stock. Scatter on plate, drizzle balsamic, yumma...

Baked salmon @RebeccaEmin
Lightly oil foil, place salmon fillet on. Add lemon juice, slices of onion & mixed herbs. Seal foil, bake 180c 25 min.

Salmon With Garlic Mash @DaintyBallerina
Fry salmon w lemon juice, red onion, tomatoes, cucumber, chillis. Mash potatoes w garlic & OO to purée.

Szechuan Pepper Salmon @goodtoweet
Coat 1side salmon darne w 1tsp crushd szechuan peppercorns & 1tsp sea salt. Dry fry, pepper side first, 3mins each side.

Cheesy Salmon Bake @jennyfoxe
Cook penne. Steam spinach & salmon darnes. Toss together & pour cheese sauce over & grate cheese on top. Bake 180c 20mins. For cheese sauce see page 71

Zesty Salmon Fillets @lisamarie20010
Mix lemon zest w cream cheese. Spread over salmon fillets. Top w breadcrumbs. Cook in lightly oiled tray 180c 25 mins.

Crusted Salmon Fillets @mduffywriter
Mix breadcrumbs, sage, pesto & finely-chopped onion & spread over salmon fillets. Bake for 180c 30 mins. Serve w salad.

Mediterranean Roast Salmon @SanyaV
Top salmon steaks w mixed chopped tomatoes, olives, OO, basil, S&P. Oven roast 25 mins. Salsa verde on the side.

Other Fish

Gizzi's Drizzled Sardines @GizziErskine
BBQ 8 butterflied sardines w salt. Heat 4tbsp EVOO w 3garlic,1red chilli,2cm ginger,1tbsp coriander(f-ch), zest 1orange til golden, drizzle.
Gizzi Erskine, chef & Television Presenter of Channel 4's *Cook Yourself Thin* (& author of the book of the same name)

Thyme For Trout @CountryLets
Slice potatoes thinly, season, sprinkle oil. Bake 220c 15 mins. Stuff trout w lemon & thyme, season, oil. Lay on spuds, cook 15min more.

Baked Trout @helen_kara
1 good-sized trout. Stuff cavity w sliced lemon&garlic, tarragon. Season. Wrap in foil w glug white wine. Bake 200c 15mins.

Gone Fishing @jennyfoxe
Rub mackerel w OO, season. Bake w oregano & red pepper flakes. Top w olives, garlic, tin tomatoes. Bake 180c until fish is flaky.

Seabass With Samphire @agnieszkasshoes
Stuff seabass w samphire, capers, butter & maybe some sliced fennel. Bake in foil 180c to be yummy & moist.

Ceviche @goodtoweet
Slice seabass fillet thinly on diagonal. Marinate in juice & zest 1 lime, 1tbsp veg oil, S&P in cool place for 15 mins. Serve immediately.

@janetravers
Fish needs to be perfectly fresh if it's to be eaten raw. Look for bright eyes and no fishy smell!

Grilled Ginger Tuna Steaks @janetravers
Marinate tuna steaks in soy sauce, OO, lime juice, grated ginger. Grill, serve w boiled rice & salad. Delicious.

Fishy Baked Eggs @CountryLets
Fry onion. Put in ramekin w 2tbsp double cream, smoked haddock. Crack egg on top, cover w gruyère, breadcrumbs & chives. Bake 160c 15min.

Any Fish Bake @abandontheherd
Wrap fish in foil w OO, lemon juice, mango, fresh herbs, S&P then grill! Yum.

[L] Simple Fish Fry @mrsredboots
Dip fish fillets in milk, then seasoned flour, then pan-fry in butter. Serve w potatoes or Chinese-style veggies.

[⏰15] Fastest Fish Supper @mollydcampbell
On parchment: diced pepper, red onion, carrot. A piece of fish, then lemon, EVOO, dill. Wrap, seal w toothpicks. Microwave 3-5 mins.

[L] Any Fish Pie @mrsredboots
Chopped white fish, parsley sauce, maybe add prawns, crab, or squid & peas etc. Top w mashed potato, bake 40 mins mod oven.

Perfect Poultry

We really do love our poultry in Ireland and the UK! We eat more chicken than any other meat, and our love affair with this versatile food shows no sign of waning.

Chicken is tasty and nutritious, but are we making the best of it? Many of us churn out the same recipes over and over again because they're easy, but our taste buds are getting bored. Many more of us only ever buy chicken breasts, but there are so many other cuts of chicken that work well in a variety of dishes. Alternatively, try using turkey or duck instead.

In the following chapter you'll find chicken and poultry dishes that can be cooked on the hob, the grill, the barbeque or in the oven. You'll find recipes using breasts, legs, wings or the entire bird. Try something new for dinner tonight.

Chicken On The Hob

Top Top Curtis Tarragon Chicken Written In Magic Secret Shorthand Richard Curtis via @emmafreud

Brwn 2 chpd onions,20 peeld garlic clvs.Add chpd chicken brst, wht wine, crèmefraîche, lots chpd tarragon. Lid, med heat.Check after 10 mins.

Richard Curtis is a screen writer, music producer, actor & director, founder of Comic Relief; Emma Freud is a script editor, producer, director of red nose day & occasional broadcaster.

One Pot Wonder @HelenRedders

Medium chicken in pot. Cover w water, white wine, 2 halved leeks, carrots & onions, bay leaf, S&P. Boil for approximately 1 hour.

Billy William's Best Entrails
@AndyStantonTM

100% organic chicken breasts, coriander, shallot, garden peas. Now chuck all that away an' eat some entrails instead.

Andy Stanton, multi-award-winning author of the *Mr Gum* books for kids.

Colette's Chilli Chicken @colettecaddle
Slice chicken boobs, pepper, spring onions, mushrooms. Stir fry. Add chpped garlic, chilli(es), dash soy, fish sauce. Add noodles, et voila!
Colette Caddle, best-selling author of 11 novels including her latest *Always On My Mind*.

Quick Creamy Chicken @mduffywriter
Fry chicken pieces w some onion & peppers, S&P, marjoram. Stir in 1tbsp flour then 230ml cream. Serve over rice.

Citrus Chicken Thighs @rosamundi
Brown chicken thighs,chopped onion,garlic.Add stock to cover,sliced orange,olives. Simmer 1hr.Boil, reduce stock.Serve w ribbon pasta.

Easy Chicken In Tomato Sauce @rosamundi
Brown onion, garlic, chicken thighs. Add 85g red lentils, 2tsp harissa paste, 1tbsp tomato purée, tin tomatoes, 450ml stock. Simmer 1 hr.

Marmalade Chicken @SarahTregear
Pan-fry chicken breast till golden. Add 280ml chicken stock, 4tbsp fine-cut marmalade, 1tsp fresh thyme. Simmer till cooked & reduced.

Chicken Fajitas @*TakeChallenge*
Fry chicken, onion, sliced red/green pepper, chilli, salt, cumin. Serve w tortillas, salsa, sour cream & chopped salad.

Grimwood's Good Chicken @*JonCG_novelist*
Marinade: dice garlic clove, fresh red chilli, 1tsp chilli flakes, 1tsp cinnamon, 1tbsp oil, mint, juice ½ lemon. Marinate chicken, fry.

Jon Courtenay Grimwood, journalist & award-winning author of *The Fallen Blade* & others

Tequila Sunrise Fajitas @*AbsoluteWrite*
Grill chicken breast sliced thin; baste w lime, tequila, garlic; serve w soft corn tortillas, mango salsa, plain yogurt.

Buffalo Wings @*chiddle84*
Mix 3tbsp melted bttr, 4tbsp tabasco, 1tbsp paprika, ½tsp each salt&cayenne peppr, ¼tsp grnd pepper. Marinade 900g chicken wings ½hr. Deep fry.

Southern Fried Chicken @*DazedPuckBunny*
Season chicken pieces in 1tsp paprika, salt & ground black pepper to taste. Roll in flour, fry in half cm hot oil for 20 mins.

Healthiest Chicken Curry @drpepperofevil
Chop & fry one onion. Add curry power & fat free yogurt to taste. Add diced chicken & cook.

Chicken À La Cox @sarajcox
Slice & bash a chicken breast until it's nice & thin. Dip in beaten egg then in mix of matzo meal & garlic salt. Shallow fry in oil. Yummo!
Sara Cox, television presenter (*The Big Breakfast*) & radio DJ

Pan-Fried Parcels @fionamulreany
Flatten a chicken breast, sprinkle w grated Parmesan & lemon rind, cover w Parma ham. Pan fry for 3-4 mins each side.

Midweek Miracle @mduffywriter
Heat leftover chicken/turkey in pan. Add tin condensed chicken soup, tin corn, cup frozen peas, cup milk & heat through. Add to cooked pasta.

Zesty Chicken Goujons @goodtoweet
Toss 1cm-thick chicken breast slices in seasoned flour, dip in beaten egg, coat w breadcrumbs, lemon zest, S&P, fry in EVOO til gold 10min.

Chicken Quesadillas @mduffywriter
Mix cooked chicken, onions, cheese & avocado. Spread between 2 flour tortillas. Fry on pan both sides. Serve in slices w sour cream.

Poulet Au Pesto @SteveHuison
Sauté 2onions til gold, add 2clove garlic,1min. 4 chick breasts, cook 4 min,turn ½ way.Add 1jar pesto,cover. Cook45 mins low.Add juice1lemon.
Steve Huison, actor best known for his role as Eddie Windass in *Coronation Street*

Sticky Chicky @PositivelyBeaut
In a saucepan: 1 sliced chicken breast, 1tbsp OO, juice of 1 orange, S&P. Cook covered until juice caramelised.

Chilli Chicken Paella @SylviaTidyHarri
Chop chicken,chilli,garlic.Fry in paella pan.Add risotto rice, peas, chickpeas, chicken stock by spoonfuls till absorbed,rice is soft.

On The BBQ Or Grill

Ginger Chilli Chicken @janegreen
Marinate 4 chicken pieces in 240ml Greek yogurt, crushed garlic clove, 1tsp each grated ginger & chilli powder. Grill. Serve w saffron rice.

Jane Green, author of 12 best-selling novels including *Jemima J* & *Promises to Keep*. A passionate foodie.

Fruity Chicken Skewers @Ailsaxburns
Marinate diced chicken w S&P, garlic, lemon juice & lime juice for 12hr. Feed onto skewers w onion, pepper, pineapple. BBQ till cooked.

Five Spice Marinade @chiddle84
Marinate chicken w soy sauce, brown sugar, sherry, white wine vinegar & 5 spice, then grill or BBQ...nom nom nom...

Shredded Chicken & Chickpeas @emilyjaneross
Rub rosemary, garlic, S&P, OO on chicken. Griddle/BBQ, shred w forks. Toss w chickpeas, toasted pinenuts & lime juice.

Thai Thighs @iknowhim
Marinate chicken thighs w star anise, lemongrass, garlic, lemon zest, chilli, coriander, white wine, OO. BBQ.

Super Speedy Satay @lisamarie20010
Mix soy sauce w chunky peanut butter. Spread over chicken breasts. Grill.

Chicken Tikka @NettieWriter
Mix large tub fat-free yogurt w 3tbsp OO, 1tbsp lemon juice, 4tbsp tikka spices. Marinate chicken breasts in mix 30mins or more. Grill/BBQ.

In The Oven

Coriander Chilli Chicken @cookinacurry
Blend 250g coriander, 2 chillis, 2 cloves garlic, 150ml yogurt, 50ml cream, lemon juice. Marinate chicken. Bake 200c 20mins or till done.
Maunika Gowardhan, a private chef/food columnist w an Indian food slot on BBC Radio 95.4FM.

Layered Chicken Bake @chiddle84
Ovenproof dish. Layers: potato slices, chicken, carrot, onion, bacon lardons, chicken stock to cover. Top w layer of potato. 180c 1hr+.

Creamy Chicken In Tomato Sauce @hainsleychariot
Fry onion & garlic. Add chopped tomatoes, cream cheese & basil. Fry chicken breasts, add to sauce. Bake 160c 25 mins.

Hot Wings @goodtoweet
Toss chicken wings in EVOO & lemon juice. Sprinkle generously w ground chilli & salt. Roast 180c for 30mins till crisp & golden.

All In One @janetravers
Roasting pan: chicken drumsticks, bay leaves, rosemary. Spray oil. 180c 30mins. Add onion, carrot, parboiled baby potatoes, 30mins more.

Simplicity @justcookit
Salt a happy hen. Roast one hour. Crisp browned skin. Allow chicken to rest. Eat w bread & a smile.
Alex Rushmer, *Masterchef* finalist 2010

Mexican Pizza @katheastman
Spread tortilla w salsa. Add stir-fried chicken, red pepper & jalapeno, spinach, grated cheese. Bake 180c 10 mins. Top w avocado slices.

Healthier Chicken Nuggets @janetravers
Cut chicken breast into strips, toss in flour, then beaten egg, then breadcrumbs. Bake 180c 20 mins.

Cheesy Chicken Parcels @NettieWriter
Split chicken breast, put a slice of cheese in middle. Wrap in slice of bacon, medium oven for 25 mins. Serve w rice & green veggies.

Luxury Baked Chicken @*JaneEFitzgerald*
Fill a chicken fillet w cream cheese, spring onions, garlic. Dip in egg & coat w breadcrumbs. Bake 180c 25mins. Yum!

Spiced Chicken Bake @*Marsha_Thomason*
Season chicken w pepper, garlic, herbs, curry pwdr, paprika. Add chpd onion,greenpepper. 180c 1hr.Add instant gravy.Bake 45mins more. Enjoy!

Marsha Thomason, British actress best known for her roles in *Las Vegas* & *Lost*.

Budget Bake @*mduffywriter*
Cook pasta. Add leftover cooked chicken/turkey, leftover veggies & tin condensed chicken soup. Oven dish & top w stuffing. 180c 30 mins.

Chicken Casserole @*rosamundi*
In casserole: chick thighs, sliced pepper, celery, lemon quarters, red onion. Glass white wine, black pepper, smoked paprika. Cook 180c 1hr.

Caribbean Roast Chicken @*LadyLittleton*
Sprinkle a chicken w Worcestershire sauce & honey. Cover.Roast 180c.10 mins before end uncover,lay pineapple slice on chicken.Oven till done.

TWEET TREATS

Simplicity Itself @jenoconnell
1 chicken breast, 1 onion, 1 can of French onion soup, 1 can of apricots. 90 mins in the oven. Done. Yum.
Jennifer O'Connell, founding editor of *TheJournal.ie*, columnist w *Sunday Business Post*, occasional broadcaster.

Mexican Turkey Bake @BlanchardAuthor
Layer refried beans, browned ground turkey, salsa, cheese, black olives. Bake 200c 15-20 minutes. Serve w tortilla chips.

Blackened Duck @Caro_Iann
Shred some ginger finely. Add juice of 4 lemons & 2tbsp honey. Mix & pour over duck breast. Bake 180c until skin blackened.

Easiest Turkey Bake @JoannaSchaff
Place strips of raw turkey breast in dish w 200mls cream & sprinkle w Parmesan. Bake at 180c till golden brown.

Turkey & Leek Pie @emilyjaneross
Sweat 6 leeks in butter 30mins. Add white wine, rosemary, thyme & cream, simmer. Add turkey & season well. Top w puffpastry. Bake180c 30mins.

Turkey Cranberry Parcels @janetravers
Spread turkey steaks liberally w good cranberry sauce. Roll, tie w twine, bay leaf on each, spray oil. Roast 180c 20mins.

Meat

Nowhere is the multi-cultural flavour of this book more evident than in these meat recipes. Although the basics of cooking remain the same, every country and every region has its own unique tastes and twists.

In this chapter you'll find appetising and unusual recipes from all over the globe. Open your mind and treat your tastebuds to the flavours of the world without ever leaving your own kitchen!

Beef

Order Take-Out @glinner
Step 1. Order Take-out...
Graham Linehan, co-Writer of *Father Ted*, *Black Books* & *The IT Crowd*.

Stovies @CountryLets
Cook 1 sliced onion in butter till soft. Add 450g diced beef, 4 large parboiled diced potatoes, S&P, 450ml beef stock. Bake 200c 50mins.

North-East English Hash @harperbrothers
Boil diced spuds. Add carrot, onion & corned beef. Crumble in stock cube & season. Simmer 20 min. Grab your toastie loaf & dig in, Bliss!
Comedy duo Rob & Darren Harper, sons of comedian Bobby Ball

Cheggers Hash @thekeithchegwin
Boil 5 spuds & 1 chopped onion till soft. Drain water. Add tin of corned beef & knob of butter. Mix together. Add pepper. Done!
Keith Chegwin, popular English television presenter.

Meatloaf @specialforksndy
Mix 5kg beef w 250ml BBQ sauce, 45g oats, 75g chopped onion & 1 egg. Form loaf, bake 190c for about 45 mins. Top w 40ml BBQ sauce.

Carla's Cheater's Meatloaf @janeaustenworld
1kg ground beef, jar med hot salsa, S&P to taste, 1tsp mustard. Mix. Oven 200c, 35-40 min.

Grilled Meatloaf @honeysock
Slice leftover meatloaf into 2cm thick slices, brush w OO, grill, turn, brush w BBQ sauce last 5 min.

Dom Joly's Trigger Happy Steak @domjoly
Mix chopped shallots, chilli, lime, brown sugar, fish sauce. Marinate steak in it. Cook steak rare, put on lettuce & pour on sauce.
Dom Joly, comedian & television personality, creator of *Trigger Happy TV*.

Hot 'N' Spicy Steak @mikelcu
Hot stir-fry sliced steak, peppers, onion, mushroom w 1tsp hot paprika & 2tsp sweet paprika. Heat off, add crème fraîche. Serve on rice.

Steak Italian Style @laurenfaith
Marinate steaks w apple cider vinegar, minced garlic, Italian seasoning, Worcestershire sauce, EVOO. Grill w sliced onions. Eat & smile.

Ginger Marinated Steak @F414
Slice raw ginger, add to 200ml soy sauce. Marinate (good) steak for 6+ hours, turning occasionally. Cook over open fire.

Veal Casserole @NETNSparents
500g diced veal, 200g diced bacon, 2 sliced celery sticks, 400g tin cream chicken soup. Bake at 160c for 2 hrs.

Mock The Wok @daraobriain
Remove packaging, pierce film lid. Heat at 180c for 25 mins. Works for lasagne, shepherd's pie, beef stew etc. etc.
Dara O'Briain, popular comedian, author & host of Mock the Week.

Casseroled Cow Cheeks @SCallejo
Brown 4 cow cheeks, cover w red wine, simmer 45 min. Add 1L beef stock, simmer 1h. Add fried onion, tomato, carrot. Stew 3hrs low heat.

Beef Crockpot @gardenfix
Beef cubes, diced tomatoes, onions, dried apricots, lemon zest, fresh ginger, cinnamon, turmeric, clove. Crockpot!

Tacos @mduffywriter
Fry 450g mince beef, onion, jalapenos, garlic, chilli powder, tin tomatoes. Load taco shells. Serve w mash avocado, sour cream, grated cheese.

Champion Chilli @thornae
Fry onion, cumin, coriander pwdr & cayenne or chilli. Add tin tomatoes, tin red kidney beans. Simmer. Add beer, chocolate (grated/powder), S&P.

Army Field Meal, Augmentation Of @destravers
Slice onion into main meal & heat in mess tin. Mix curry powder into paste, add to main. Go! Warning: cook to windward of enemy positions. Yo!
Colonel Desmond Travers, one of the authors of the United Nations Fact Finding Mission on the Gaza Conflict, or 'Goldstone Report'.

Lamb

Cypriot Kleftiko @philknoxville
Seal lamb shanks in tinfoil w tomatoes, onions, 1 cinnamon stick, 1 bay leaf, OO. Slow roast 140c 2-3hrs.
Phil 'Knoxville' Hasted – stand-up comedian, actor & performer of twisted magic.

Lamb Shank Casserole @mrsredboots
Brown lamb shanks then cook in slow cooker w onion, carrot, tinned tomatoes, tinned white beans, seasoning.

Lamb Stew For Two @digital_times
Dice 1 carrot, onion, celery, spud, garlic, chilli. Fry gently in pot w 2 lamb chops. Add 1 handful barley. Cover w water. Simmer 2 hrs.

Meltingly Good Roast Leg Of Lamb
@goodtoweet
Mash 5 anchovy fillets w juice & zest ½ lemon, 1tbsp thyme, S&P. Rub all over leg lamb. Roast lamb 180c 1-1.5 hrs then rest 20mins.

Cojones Al Ajo *@davidgilray*
Skin, slice & gently fry ram or stallion testicles in OO w garlic. An aphrodisiac. One for the men, obviously!

Greek Burgers *@NettieWriter*
Add mint, cinnamon, coriander & beaten egg to lamb mince. Form into patties w a cube of feta in middle. Grill until cooked.

Shepherd's Pie *@janetravers*
Brown lamb mince.Remove. Sauté onion&rosemary in juices.250ml stock, reduce.Return lamb&passata to pan. Simmer ages.Top w mash, grill.

Pork

Top Sausage Pie *@emmafreud*
Pie dish... Raw sausage meat at bottom, layer of ketchup, layer of grated cheddar, layer of puff pastry. 180c 30-40mins till golden brown.
Emma Freud is a script editor, producer, director of Red Nose Day & occasional broadcaster.

Pork With Tarragon Cream @DaveBartlett1
Fry f-ch onions, mushrooms, add tarragon & 250ml double cream. Cook till thickened. Top pork loin steaks, wrap in foil. Roast 180c 20mins.

Tweatballs @SCallejo
Whiz ½ onion, 1 garlic, 2 eggs, breadcrumbs, grated nutmeg, salt. Add to 1kg minced pork. Form balls & fry until brown.

Keith's Crubeens @keithpbarry
Pig's feet boiled – straight on the plate w cabbage which has been glazed w brown sauce. (As cooked on *The Restaurant* on RTE 1)

Keith Barry, magician & illusionist, internationally known on television & in theatres.

Pork Skewers @gardenfix
Marinate pork loin cubes in OO, lemon juice, garlic. Thread on skewers. Mushrooms, peppers, baby tomatoes optional. BBQ.

Dijon Pork @goodtoweet
Brown 6 thick rounds pork fillet & sliced onion in hot butter & S&P. Add glass white wine, tsp Dijon mustard. Cover. Med oven 15 mins.

Tardis Tortilla @Paul_Cornell
Grate parboiled potatoes into pan. Fry. Add egg, bacon, cheese, & onions if a weirdo. Careful w the flip.
Paul Cornell, novelist, comics & TV writer, notably for *Doctor Who, Coronation Street* & *Primeval*.

Sausage & Onion Parcels @NettieWriter
Layer 3 filo pastry sheets w melted butter. Cooked sausage & onion relish in middle. Twist:make parcel. Brush w melted butter. 180c 15 mins.

Ham & Leek Gratin @jennyfoxe
Layer sliced potatoes, sliced leek & ham. Pour 280ml cream over. Grate cheese on top. 180c 40mins.

Egg & Pancetta Hash @Candida6
Boil new potatoes & leafy greens, crush. Sauté onion, 3 garlic cloves, pancetta in OO. Add to crushed spuds & greens. Top w poached egg.

Maple Mustard Sausages @chiddle84
Marinate sausages in 3tbsp maple syrup, 1tbsp Dijon mustard, S&P for 1 hour. Bake 180c 30mins. Yum w oodles of mash.

Bo' Selecta Dogs @LeighFrancis
I don't cook. Take 8 hot dogs in brine, heat them up in a pan. Put them in a hot dog bun, add mustard & ketchup. Eat!
Leigh Francis, English comedy performer most famous for his comedy series Bo' Selecta!

Quiche Lorraine @dinkydenman
Sauté onion, peppers, bacon. Add to 3 eggs, 250ml milk&cream, S&P, mixed herbs, Gruyère cheese.Mix. Pour into pastry case. Bake 180c 40 mins.

Comfort Hash @stallionbreaker
Sauté 450g sausage meat & bunch chopped kale. Boil 900g potatoes w salt 20min. Mash all together w splash of milk. Bowl of comfort.

Savoury Bread & Butter Pudding @helen_kara
Slice, butter stale bread.Layer in dish w chopped onion & ham.Nearly cover w 3:1 beaten eggs & milk, S&P.Top w grated cheese.180c till gold.

Sausage Casserole @chiddle84
Simmer tin tomatoes w garlic, peppers, onion, other veg. Partly cook sausages. All into casserole dish. Add grated cheese. 45mins 150c.

Best Keep It Short @CalumBest
Honey glazed ribs & coleslaw! X
Calum Best, TV personality, reality show contestant & fashion model.

Dublin Coddle @mduffywriter
Boil 8 whole sausages, 8 slices salty bacon.Reduce heat.Add 2 onions, 2 carrots, 8 potatoes all diced.S&P, parsley.Simmer till spuds tender.

Creamy Cajun Pork @mduffywriter
Coat strips of pork in cajun seasoning & fry w onion, red pepper, garlic. Stir in tomato purée & double cream. Serve over rice.

Poached Egg & Parma Ham @AnneMarieT123
Wrap Parma ham round asparagus, season & coat w OO. Roast in medium oven for 15mins. Serve w poached egg & a squeeze of lemon juice.

Flammekueche @joecleere
Roll puffpastry 1-2mm thin as pizza.Top: créme fraîche, onion, bacon bits, mozzarella, brie. Bake 180c max 20mins.
Joe Cleere, musician, currently supporting Status Quo.

Chorizo Hash @*Hardyduncan*
Sauté onion, carrot, celery & garlic w chorizo. Add green lentils & a tomato. Simmer 20mins. Season! Serve w poached egg.

Layered Ham & Cheese Pie @*SCallejo*
Line tin w pastry. Layer slices cheese, ham, dates, bacon. Repeat. Close top layer w pastry. Bake 180c 30 mins.

Pork Marsala @*hprw*
Fry pork chops & apple slices until nearly done. Slosh in Marsala & reduce. Eat w crusty granary bread & green salad. Mmm!

Chops 'N' Capers @*goodtoweet*
Season pork chops well. Fry in EVOO on hot pan till well coloured & just cooked. Add handful of capers, 1 min.

The Fry To End All Fries @*rebeccaebrown*
Fry gammon steaks. Serve w fried sliced potato, fried chopped onion, fried egg & fried sliced pineapple.

Greens, Eggs & Ham *@goodtoweet*
Make a soft omelette & fill w tender steamed asparagus, diced ham & lots of Parmesan. Serve w plain boiled new potatoes.

Better Than Beans On Toast *@MJulieMiller*
Warm a tin of butter beans in home-made tomato sauce w chunks of pan-fried ham off the bone. Serve w good, warm bread. For tomato sauce see page 106

Pork Casserole *@Lyvit*
Dice pork & roll in flour. Add onion, celery, apple & stock to cover. All in casserole dish & top w garlic bread. Med oven 40mins.

Ghetto Frittata *@myownbiggestfan*
Chop some bacon & green onion, grate 80g cheese, mix w three eggs & seasoning. Fry 5 min each side.

Pasta & Rice Dishes

Where would we be without pasta? The go-to cupboard staple for quick and easy dinners, lunches or salad ingredients, pasta comes in dozens of varieties and is endlessly versatile. It's cheap, keeps well and cooks in minutes, providing a terrific base for any meal.

Yet many of us are guilty of taking this glorious foodstuff and smothering it in shop-bought sauces because of lack of time or inclination to do anything different. Even on those most harried of days you'll find a recipe in this chapter for a sauce or pasta dish that will be ready in the amount of time it takes to boil a pot of spaghetti.

Rice is another staple that we take for granted, a terrific food that comes in a number of varieties to suit different types of dish. Gluten and dairy free, rice can be eaten by almost everyone.

Create some new family traditions with these great pasta and rice recipes.

Pasta Dishes
Tomato-Based Sauces

Puttanesca Pasta Sauce *@Tracy_Chevalier*
Onion, garlic, olives, capers, anchovies, chilli flakes, tomato sauce, parsley. Combine, reduce, eat.
Tracy Chevalier, award-winning author of several novels including *The Girl with a Pearl Earring*.

Creamy Red Wine Sauce *@gcolliasuzuki*
Fry chopped onion & garlic, add red wine & reduce. Add tin chopped tomatoes. Add fresh basil & 2 dollops of cream cheese.

Vine Tomato Sauce @HazelKLarkin
Heat 4tbsp EVOO, cook 1 bulb crushed garlic, add 15 vine tomatoes, skinned & chopped & herbs (lots). Simmer 30 mins.

Speediest Tomato Sauce @abigailrieley
Take tin of plum tomatoes & heat quickly for around 5 minutes w dash balsamic & fresh basil. Serve w Parmesan & wholewheat pasta.
Abigail Rieley, journalist & author of *Death on the Hill*.

Hot Pasta Salad @janetravers
Roast cherry vine tomatoes w splash balsamic vinegar 200c 10 mins. Mix w cooked pasta, serve on a bed of salad leaves & fresh basil.

Anchovy Pasta Sauce @robinbogg
Onion, leek, dried chillies, anchovies, tin tomatoes. Reduce. Stir in lemon juice, garlic, purple sprouting broccoli.

Prawn & Chorizo Pasta @wendytalksback
Boil spaghetti. Fry chorizo, sunblush tomatoes, chilli & onion in oil & butter. Add prawns. On pasta, add basil leaves & lime juice. Enjoy!
Wendy Austin, talkback anchor for BBC Radio Ulster

Zingy Linguine @goodtoweet
Add anchovy fillets, capers, ground dried chilli to your basic tomato pasta sauce. Serve w linguine. Sprinkle w breadcrumbs fried in EVOO.

L

Chilli Chicken Penne @RupertHill
Fry onion, chicken, garlic, 2 chillis & chorizo in OO till yum, then add chopped tomatoes & tomato purée. Stir into penne. So simple!
Rupert Hill, actor best known for his role as Jamie Baldwin in *Coronation Street*.

L

Cheesy Pasta Bake @megfdavies
Soften pancetta & chopped tomatoes in OO. Add basil, diced mozzarella, Parmesan. Mix w cooked penne, top more Parmesan. Bake hot till brown.

Sticky Pasta @kwazana
Heat OO, fry garlic, pitted olives & anchovies. Add tomato paste & fry until it sticks. Serve on bucatini pasta w Parmesan.

L

Spagbol @Richardm56
500g beef mince, tin tomatoes, tom purée, splash of stock, ½bottle red wine, mixd herbs, chopped onion, clove garlic. Simmer 2hrs, add glass sherry.
Richard Madeley, enormously-popular television presenter of *Richard & Judy* fame.

L

Chunky Cheese'n'Chorizo Sauce
@chiddle84

Cook pasta. Fry onion, chilli, garlic, S&P, chunks chorizo. Add chopped tomatoes & single cream. Simmer til thick. Sprinkle w cheese. NOM.

Easy Creamy Pasta Sauce *@SCallejo*

Mix tub mascarpone w tin of tomato purée or chopped tomatoes. Heat, stir until creamy. Add herbs. Mix w cooked pasta.

[V] [L]

My Nonna's Pasta Sauce *@rachelleskovac1*

Fry onion & lamb blade in OO. Remove onion. Add passata, basil & season. Cook for 3hrs at least.

Rachel Leskovac, actress best known for her role as Natasha in *Coronation Street*.

[L]

Other Pasta Dishes

Pete's Pasta *@paulakahumbu*

Grate 5 courgettes. Fry w 1 chopped onion, 2 cloves garlic, squeeze lemon, salt, OO. Add to cooked spaghetti & grated cheese.

Paula Kahumbu, ecologist, conservationist & children's author.

[V] [⏰] [L]

Parikian's Perfect Pasta @LevParikian
Oil on low heat. Chop garlic & chilli fine. Add to oil. Do not burn! Boil water. Pasta in. Cook. Check. Drain. Mix. Parmesan? Of course.

No Cook Pasta Sauce @LevParikian
Beat 100g goat's cheese, juice & grated zest of 1 lemon, glug OO, black pepper, handful basil. Add to freshly-cooked pasta.

Pasta with Prawns @ClodaghMMurphy
Cook spaghetti or pasta of choice. Fry peeled king prawns in a little OO & harissa paste. Mix together.
Clodagh Murphy, author of *The Disengagement Ring* & *Girl In A Spin*.

Spaghetti Carbonara @TheGlutton
Fry some pancetta. Mix 100ml cream, 60g Parmesan, 1 egg & black pepper. Stir through cooked pasta & pancetta. The heat will cook the egg.

Perfect Carbonara @clarebalding1
For perfect spaghetti carbonara use double cream & the secret ingredient: a whole pat of Boursin cheese!
Clare Balding, television presenter & sports journalist

Turkey Carbonara @JackyHSF
Fry bacon strips, onion, turkey strips, mushrooms. Add to cooked pasta. Stir in 150ml cream, 50g grated Parmesan, 300ml yogurt. Heat.

Pat's Packed Pasta @patomahony1
Onion, mushrooms, garlic, tomatoes, black pepper, oregano, smoky bacon sauce, crème fraîche, prawns, frozen peas. Pasta, pesto. Yum!
Pat O'Mahony, Irish television & radio personality.

Spaghetti With Chilli & Garlic @Deborahhollamby
Gently fry lots of garlic & chilli in best OO. Boil spaghetti, drain, toss in garlic & chilli. Add freshly-ground black pepper.

Pasta With Pine Nuts & Pesto @FictionWitch
Sauté pine nuts & chopped ham. Add rocket pesto & crème fraîche. Serve w pasta.

Easiest Mid-Week Meal @janetravers
Boil penne 5 mins. Add ham, broccoli, frozen peas. Finish cooking pasta, drain. Toss in OO, lemon zest, juice ½ lemon. Generous Parmesan.

Tarragon Cream Sauce @christinemosler
Chop asparagus & fry in butter w garlic. Add oyster mushrooms, Dijon mustard, glass white wine, 250ml cream, tarragon. Stir into pasta.

Pappardelle with Figs & Chilli @guillorybe
6 figs, sliced. Sauté 2 mins w 1 red chilli pepper & honey. Serve over fresh pappardelle w a little cream & lemon zest.

Sienna Guillory, actress best known for her role in *Resident Evil: Apocalypse.*

Broccoli Linguine @goodtoweet
Sauté 1 clove crushed garlic in 2tbsp EVOO. Add 4 anchovies, 200g steamed purple sprouting broccoli, S&P, lemon juice. Toss w linguine & EVOO.

Mac & Cheese @janetravers
Boil macaroni 5 mins. Add peas, broccoli, ham. Finish cooking all, drain. Into ovenproof dish, cheese sauce over, sliced tomato on top, grill. For cheese sauce see page 71

Creamy Chicken Pasta @NettieWriter
Sauté chicken, peppers, babycorn, mangetout, onion, courgettes, mushrooms. Mix 1packet Boursin, 1 carton single cream, splash milk. Serve on pasta.

TWEET TREATS 111

Feta & Artichoke Pasta @helen_kara
Fry red onion & sliced red chilli till soft. Add cubed feta, sliced artichoke hearts. Stir into pasta, drizzle w OO.

Courgette Cream @florNEWS
Swish some garlic, scallion, courgette (grated) in butter. Add 250ml cream, pour over pasta. Season well, Parmesan, vino bianco...
Flor McCarthy, News Reporter at the Foreign Unit, RTE news.

Sauce for Stuffed Pasta @helen_kara
Fry sliced shallots, garlic, mushrooms & chopped parsley. Add white wine, reduce. Season. Add crème fraîche.

Vegetable Pasta Pesto @RebeccaEmin
Fry chopped courgette, aubergine, pepper, mushroom, onion, garlic in OO. Cook pasta bows. Mix together & add red pesto.

Spaghetti With Tuna & Leek @VoiceOverVic
Sweat leek 5 mins while cooking spaghetti. Add cooked pasta to leek w lime juice, can of tuna, cup of fromage frais & seasoning.

Prawn Pasta with Garlic & Chilli
@Cornflowerbooks

Sweat garlic & chilli flakes in OO, add pine nuts & let brown. Then throw in prawns, lemon juice & spring onions. Serve on pasta.

L

Creamy Leek & Bacon Sauce
@dorristheloris

Fry leek & bacon till soft. Add enough stock to make it soupy & let it stew for 20 mins. Stir in pepper & dbl cream. Pasta sauce!

Courgette & Garlic Pasta *@aoifemcl*
Slice courgette finely, fry slowly w chopped garlic until soft & almost transparent. Season. Serve w pasta & Parmesan.

L

Pasta With Salmon *@MJulieMiller*
Cook 100g pasta, drain. Stir in good squeeze of lemon juice & 50ml cream. Season. Add sliced smoked salmon & handful of rocket.

L

10 Mins Dins *@Cerise_J*
To drained pasta add red pesto, tinned tuna, jar of artichoke hearts, black olives, grated Parmesan & black pepper.

L

Rice, Noodle & Couscous Dishes

Bean & Bacon Risotto *@MiriamWakerly*
Gently sauté onion.Add bacon bits/pancetta, broad beans, button mushrooms.Add Arborio rice.Add stock by spoonfuls, cooking till all absorbed.

Broccoli & Bacon Risotto *@New2WritingGirl*
Heat butter, add risotto rice. Add veg stock slowly till absorbed. Then fry leek, onion, broccoli & bacon. Mix & add grated Parmesan.

Clonakilty Pudding Risotto *@manaboutcouch*
Sauté onion, garlic, chorizo.Add Arborio rice, vermouth, veg stock, cook till absorbed.Top: Clonakilty pudding, Parmesan, steamed asparagus.

@manaboutcouch
Tip: Cook the Clonakilty pudding first & fold into the risotto just before serving, otherwise it'll turn to mush!

Red Pesto Risotto *@helen_kara*
Fry onion, add risotto rice & stir, add stock slowly. When done, stir in red pesto to taste. Top w caramelised onions.

Easiest Vegetable Risotto @RebeccaEmin
L Fry chopped onion. Add any other chopped veg. Add veg stock if you have it, herbs & water if not. Add rice & simmer until rice soft.

Mushroom Risotto @janetravers
V Soak dried mushrooms.Sauté onions, fresh mushrooms, garlic.Add dried mushrooms, Madeira wine.Reduce.Add Arborio rice.Add stock til absorbed.

Risotto With Prawns @robinbogg
L Cook Arborio rice in stock,fish sauce,chilli,ginger,coconut milk (spoonful at a time till absorbed). Stir in prawns, lime juice, coriander.

Risotto With Almonds @hmhunt
L Fry celery, onions, garlic, fresh ginger & other veg. Add rice & stock. Simmer until liquid absorbed. Add toasted almonds.

Risotto with Artichoke Hearts @helen_kara
L Fry shallots.Stir in risotto rice, veg stock slowly till absorbed.Near end add sliced artichoke hearts, f-ch parsley, Parmesan, S&P.

Fried Rice *@haydn_p_jones*
Sauté finely chopped onion/garlic in wok w oil, soy sauce, vegetable stock cube, prawns/chicken. Add boiled rice.

Cheats' Fried Rice *@mduffywriter*
Fry leftover rice in OO. Add turmeric, salt, black pepper. Finely chop onions, carrots, peppers (any veg), fry, add to rice.

Bok Choi Stir Fry With Chestnut Mushrooms *@richardwiles*
Stir fry sliced chestnut mushrooms, spring onions, chilli, garlic, red pepper, quartered bok choi. Add fish & plum sauce. Serve w noodles.

Spinach & Feta Couscous *@LaCaffeinata*
Boil 4 cups of frozen spinach in ½L chicken broth, add 1 cup of couscous, let simmer for 10min. Top w tiny pieces of feta.

Vegetarian & Vegan Dishes

If you're vegetarian or vegan you know the importance of eating a richly-varied and well-balanced diet in order to get all the essential nutrients, but you're probably stuck in a rut of eating the same meals over and over. On the following pages you'll find a number of simple, tasty and nutritious meals from all over the world to liven up your repertoire.

Perhaps you're not vegetarian or vegan yourself, but like to have meat-free meals occasionally – if you could only think what to cook. Or perhaps your vegetarian friends are sick of being served a plate of uninspired vegetables and you've been presented with this book as a large hint!

Cheese is a minefield for many vegetarians. Not all omnivores are aware that some cheeses (such as Parmesan) are unsuitable for vegetarians as they are made with rennet. The following recipes feature cheeses that are completely acceptable to vegetarians, sometimes specifying vegetarian versions of regular cheeses, which are available in specialist shops. Always read the label! Likewise, not all vegetarians eat eggs, but these recipes assume that they do.

Some of the ingredients listed such as Vecon (a concentrated gluten-free vegetable stock) are available in specialist food shops; others can be found in your local supermarket if you're lucky.

Vegetarian Recipes
Cheese-Based Dishes

Chilli Paneer @*samfoxcom*
Sauté3tbsp each garlic,tom sauce,1tbsp chilli sauce,3grn chilli,3onion,soy sce,S&P.Add cubes paneer coatd w1tsp cornflr,2tsp flour.Fry gold.
Samantha Fox, singer, entertainer & model.

Goat's Cheese & Vegetable Roast @*27storybuilding*
Marinate peppers, squash, aubergine, red onion, courgette, goat's cheese & cherry tomatoes in balsamic vinegar & rosemary. Roast.

Butternut Squash & Red Pepper Casserole @*JackyHSF*
700g diced butrnut squash, 1 red pepper, 2tsp OO, garlic, chpd parsley, rosemary, S&P. In gratin dish, top w vegetarian Parmesan. 200c 1hr.

Roulé Cheese Stuffed Mushrooms @*ClaireAllan*
How about Portobello mushrooms, stuffed w Roulé cheese, coated in breadcrumbs & baked at 200c for 30 minutes?
Claire Allan, best-selling author of *Rainy Days and Tuesdays* among others.

Potato & Halloumi Bake *@CountryLets*
Roast sweet potatoes, potatoes, red & yellow peppers, red onion, garlic, oil & pepper 200c 20 mins. Add slices of Halloumi, bake 15min.

Ring The Bells *@fuelthefighter*
Stuff a hollowed-out bell pepper w salsa, 90g black beans, diced jalapeno, 2tbsp vegetarian cheddar. Bake 190c 15-20 min.

Nut Roast *@helen_kara*
Chop any nuts, grate any veg & hard cheese. Add 1tbsp tomato purée & enough beaten egg to combine. Herbs. Season, press into tin, bake firm.

Savoury Pancakes *@helen_kara*
Roll ready-made pancakes round defrosted frozen spinach, grated feta & a little freshly-grated nutmeg. Warm through in oven.

Easy Bean Bake *@austen_addict*
Layer steamed string beans & mushroom soup w crushed garlic, veggie Parmigiano cheese in oiled baking dish. 180c till bubbly.
Laurie Viera Rigler, author of Confessions of a Jane Austen Addict & Rude Awakenings of a Jane Austen Addict

Vegetarian Lasagne @hprw
Roast onions, peppers, butternut squash, whole garlic cloves. Cheese sauce w pinch cumin. Layer up w lasagne sheets, bake 180c 30-35mins!

For cheese sauce see page 71

Veggie Cholesterol Special @KateWritesBooks
Stone 1 avocado. Fill gap w Boursin/soft cheese & pecans/walnuts. Cover w veggie Cheddar. Grill till melted, eat w melba toast.

Baked Goat's Cheese @McTheMac
Spread some marmalade (or cranberry sauce) on top of goat's cheese. 5 mins in hot oven & serve w crusty bread.

Winter Tart @seo01
Dice & roast large beetroot & butternut squash. Mix w feta & pinenuts. Put on a large square of pre-rolled puff pastry. Bake 180c for 20m.

Tallegio Tart @emmafreud
Roll out puff pastry & prick all over w fork. Top w caramelised onions, tallegio cheese, thyme. Bake medium oven 10 mins. Stunning!

Emma Freud is a script editor, producer, director of Red Nose Day & occasional broadcaster.

120 TWEET TREATS

Student Special @MikeyUnderwood
Mashed potato, tomato soup, cheese. Put mash in bowl & make hole in centre. Pour in soup & grate cheese on top.
Mikey Underwood, British Television presenter & reality show contestant.

Egg-Based Dishes

Classic Tortilla @conor_pope
Onion diced, 4 spuds diced & parboiled, OO, 6 eggs, salt. Fry onions & potatoes, add eggs, fry, flip, fry.
Conor Pope, consumer affairs journalist for *The Irish Times*, author of *Stop Wasting Your Money*.

Frittata @CafeFresh
Roast sliced onion, garlic, potato in oven. Beat 8 eggs, mix w the cooked veg, season. Bake in dish for 20 minutes medium oven.

Pease Pudding @rebeccaebrown
Split peas, chopped onion, cover w water. Boil, then simmer till soft. Liquidise, crack in an egg. Ovenproof dish, bake 180c 30 mins.

Spinach Gratin @juxtabook
Cooked spinach into gratin dish. Make 2 hollows. Crack an egg into each. Top w 1tbsp natural yogurt, grated cheese. 180c 20 mins.

Indian Omelette @JosaYoung
Slice green chilli & onion finely & fry until soft in a little butter. Add beaten egg to make an Indian omelette.

L

Rock On Egg & Chips @TheBobbyBall
Peel & slice tatties, fry in hot oil til golden. Fry eggs in hot pan, cook till yolks at desired runniness & serve w side of choice. :-)

L

Migas @honeysock
In EVOO sauté 75g each peppers & onions, add 75g chopped corn tortillas. Push aside. Scramble 6 eggs, add cheese, mix all together =>YUM

Spinach & Tomato Tart @helen_kara
Line blind-baked pastry case w steamed, drained spinach, layer sliced tomatoes. Top w beaten egg & cream, blk ppr, grated cheese. Bake.

Vegetable Tortilla @samatredmag
Fry onion, red pepper, mushrooms, sweetcorn. Add boiled new potatoes, saffron, paprika, 4 eggs. Fry slowly. Flip tortilla. Fry more!
Sam Baker, editor of *Red* magazine, author of *The Stepmothers Support Group* & *To My Best Friends.*

Mushroom Eggs Benedict @christinemosler
Top butter-fried Portobello mushroom w FR poached egg. Mix crème fraîche, dijon, lemon juice, capers, S&P together & pour over.

Other Vegetarian Recipes

Autumn Warmer @MrNickKnowles
Take small pumpkin, cut top off, take seeds out, replace w a knob of butter, Cajun spice, S&P. Microwave 6 mins.
Nick Knowles, British TV presenter, writer & director

Mushroom Medley @CountryLets
Fry wild mushrooms, chestnut mushrooms, onion, garlic in butter until cooked. Squeeze of lemon, serve w rice, sprinkle w parsley.

Leeks En Croute @helen_kara
Wrap each cleaned leek in ready-rolled puff pastry. Seal & glaze w milk or egg. Bake 190c 20-30 mins till gold/soft.

BBQ Veggie Pouches @honeysock
Toss together sliced mushrooms, peppers, onions, carrots w OO & BBQ sauce. Seal in pocket of foil, grill or BBQ.

Dhal @helen_kara
Cook lentils w turmeric & sliced ginger. Fry onion seeds, sliced garlic & chilli in lots of ghee. Stir into lentils. Season.

Leek & Potato Pie @CountryLets
Place circle of puff pastry in bottom gratin dish. Top w sliced potato & leek, S&P. Another circle of puff, brush w egg. Bake 200c 50mins.

Vegan Recipes

Sweet Potato Gumbo @TristanGemmill
Sauté onions, garlic & chilli in pan. Add boiled sweet potatoes, red kidney beans & coriander. Serve on rice.

Vegetable Wontons @Cidtalk
Fill vegan wonton pastry w roast squash, fresh ginger, lemon zest, fresh thyme, basil & sage.Parcels. Brown & steam for a few mins – delish!

Aubergine Mash @goodtoweet
Roast 1 aubergine 200c 30min. Peel, mash, add 4tbsp lemon juice, 4tbsp tahini, 1tsp minced garlic, S&P, 2tbsp EVOO. Scatter coriander.

Butternut Squash Risotto @AlanCarr
Cut up a roast butternut squash. Cook some risotto rice then add the diced squash. Season.
Alan Carr, stand up comedian & TV presenter.

Ratatouille @HazelKLarkin
Cook 1 onion till soft. Add aubergine, courgette, green pepper. Cook till softened. Add tomato sauce, herbs, salt. Simmer 40 mins.

For tomato sauce see page 106

Refried beans @helen_kara
Fry onions, green peppers, garlic. Add 1tsp ground cumin, 2tsp ground coriander, pre-cooked pinto beans, salt. Mash.

Baked Peppers @helen_kara
Fill halved red peppers w cherry tomatoes, button mushrooms & peeled garlic cloves. Drizzle tamari, OO. Bake 180c til soft.

Curried Sweet Potato Rounds @paulakahumbu
Slice boiled sweet potato into rounds, coat in curry powder & shallow fry till brown. Enjoy hot w homemade tomato chutney.
Paula Kahumbu, ecologist, conservationist & children's author.

Aubergine Curry @HazelKLarkin
Halve 6 baby aubergines lengthways. Top w masala paste, fried onion, 3tbsp green curry paste & can coconut milk. Cover & simmer till done.

Chilli Sin Carne @jacr13
Sauté leek, carrot, onion, garlic; add chilli powder & cumin, can of kidney beans, can of tomatoes, tbsp vecon, tsp mustard. Cook through.

Vegetable Stew @HazelKLarkin
Sauté onion. Add juice of 85g grated ginger, tin tomatoes, chilli paste. Boil. Simmer 5 mins, add 2 chpd sweet pots & half cauli. Cook 15 mins.

Chilli Rice & Beans @jacr13
1 tin Mexican beans, 1 tin chopped tomatoes w chilli, add basil, herbs, chilli powder. Heat together, serve w rice.

Curried Spuds & Chick Peas @mikelcu
New potatoes, can of curried chick peas in pan. Cook until potatoes are cooked. Serve hot or cold.

Spiced Lentils @jennyfoxe
Sauté 1 onion & 1 clove garlic, stir in 1tsp curry powder & 175g lentils. Add 375 ml vegetable stock. Cook for 20 mins.

Potato Curry @jacr13
For 2: fry 50g red curry paste w oil 30 secs, add 400ml coconut milk, diced spuds, chopped onion & mushrooms. Cook till spuds are tender.

Smoked Tofu Sandwich @sgwarnog
Slice smoked tofu, marinate in soy sauce, fry in hot oil. Serve in toasted bread w mustard.

Vegan Desserts

Vegan Chocolate Tart @PETA
Meltd marg,25 crushd vegan choc cookies.Stir.Dish. Fridge30min.Blend560g soft tofu,140g semisweet meltd vegan choc chips.In crust,chill 2hrs.

People for the Ethical Treatment of Animals (PETA), with more than 2 million members & supporters, is the largest animal rights organisation in the world.

Vegan Bananaberry 'Ice Cream' @DaynaR
Blitz 3 quartered frozen bananas. Add 150g frozen berries, drizzle vegan chocolate syrup, process again. Squish w hands if necessary. Serve.

Frozen Banana Shake @olivosartstudio
2 frozen bananas in food processor, raw cacao, dash of vanilla, dash of cinnamon (dash of rum optional). Blend.

TWEET TREATS 127

Banana Mango Blitz @olivosartstudio
Two frozen bananas, 1 frozen mango, all in blender = raw vegan ice cream!

Spreads, Dips & Preserves

So, you have people dropping over unexpectedly and you think you've nothing to offer them? Well, check out this chapter for some terrific dips, spreads and salsas that you can throw together from whatever is in your store cupboard. All you need is five minutes warning and access to a food processor.

Many of the following recipes are vegetarian, vegan, gluten-free or all of the above, solving all of your hosting dilemmas. Even better, most of them don't require any cooking.

Come to think of it, there's no need to wait for unexpected guests. Just break out the food processor and get cracking! Just make sure you always have an emergency packet of crackers on hand for when the mood strikes.

Spreads
Savoury

Walnut Pâté @BoyGeorge
2 cups walnuts, 1 chopped red pepper, 2 sticks celery, dash of Braggs Aminos, S&P, parsley; blend in food processor.
Boy George, singer-songwriter, DJ, fashion designer and photographer.

Bean Pâté @CafeFresh
Sauté onion, garlic, 200g root vegetables & 1 diced chilli until soft. Add 150g cooked pinto beans. Blend & season.

Mackerel Pâté @goodtoweet
Mash together 2 fillets smoked mackerel, 1 grated shallot, 3tbsp melted butter, chopped parsley, lemon zest, pepper. Press into dish.

Zesty Smoked Mackerel Pâté @nicolamorgan
Smoked mackerel, cream cheese, juice & zest lemon & lime, chopped onion, horseradish, black pepper, paprika. Mash & eat!
Nicola Morgan, award-winning Author (of *Wasted* & others) & speaker re: books, teenage fiction, brains, publishing.

Anchovy Butter @Gargarin
1 tin anchovies, 125g butter. Liquidize & add black pepper. Spread on hot toast, yum! Keeps well in the fridge.

Sardine Spread @SCallejo
100g natural spread cheese, 1 tin grilled red peppers, 2 tins sardines. Whizz until creamy.

Poached Salmon Spread @austenonly
Small piece poached salmon. Add mayo, lemon juice, black pepper, salt. Whiz in blender. Spread on sliced, toasted baguette.

Garlic Brie @NettieWriter
Purée 8 cloves baked garlic, 180g black pitted olives, 60ml OO. Add to 225g melted brie. Blend, cool in fridge.

Whitebean Pâté @JoTreggiari
400g can whitebeans, squeeze lemon juice, 60ml OO, 10g parsley, 1 garlic clove. Purée, spread on sliced french bread.
Jo Treggiari, author of children's book *Feltus Ovalton* & acclaimed teen novel *Ashes, Ashes*

Pea Purée @goodtoweet
Sweat ¼ onion in butter, add 100g cooked peas, S&P, squeeze of lemon juice. Blend till smooth, add handful chopped mint. Great w fish.

Garlic Pea Purée @LevParikian
Roast head garlic, squeeze out. Simmer frozen peas (plenty). Season. Whizz all w OO. Spread on small toasts or use as dip.

Herb Butter @CountryLets
Mix butter w parsley, sage, thyme, garlic. Particularly great w poultry, but can be used w anything.

Garlic Butter @LaCaffeinata
Wrap garlic bulb in foil, roast in oven 200c 30min until it's mushy. Mix w 225g butter, add S&P.

Sweet

Honey Spread @simoncowan
One part tahini to two parts honey (or to taste), mix it in a small glass. Makes fabulous spread for pita bread. Better than peanut butter.

Honey Butter @cathyby
Let unsalted butter soften at room temp, beat in honey to taste. Scrummy on fresh baked bread.

Preserves
Savoury

Chilli Oil Chips @fionalooney
Add dried chillies & peppercorns to OO, leave for a week. Use peeler to cut thin strips of spud. Deep fry in the oil.
Fiona Looney, Irish columnist, playwright, scriptwriter & media personality.

@janetravers
Remember when you're preserving to use clean jars, sterilised in an oven 180c for 20mins. Don't add cold food to hot jars or vice versa!

Dill Green Tomatoes @janeaustenworld
Save the pickle juice from your dill pickle jar. Add end-of-season green tomatoes. Pickle them in the juice. Yum.

Coconut Chilli Chutney @SanyaV
Can creamed coconut. Add chillies, chopped ginger, garlic, coriander, mint to taste. Add salt, pinch sugar, squeeze lime. Mix.

Redcurrant Chutney @TheDailySpud
Bring 800g redcurrants, 400g sugar, 4tbsp red wine vinegar, 1tsp grnd ginger, 1tsp grnd allspice to the boil. Simmer 40 mins then bottle.

Oven-Dried Tomatoes @paulakahumbu
Sprinkle S&P & herbs on tomato halves, dry for 3 days in slow oven. Seal in jars w sliced garlic & OO.
Paula Kahumbu, ecologist, conservationist & children's author.

Relish for Grilled Chicken @LibertyLndnGirl
Slice kernels off corncob. Mix w 2 chopped tomatoes, splash EVOO, S&P, handful cilantro & 1 chilli chopped.
Sasha Wilkins, English style journalist, editor & broadcaster, creator of multi-award winning lifestyle blog **LibertyLondonGirl.**

Sweet

Strawberry Jam @CountryLets
1kg strawbs, 750g jam sugar, mix leave overnight, heat gently until sugar melted. Add juice 1 lemon. Rolling boil, 8mins, cool 15min & pot

Redcurrant Jelly @CountryLets
1kg redcurrants, heat in pan till soft. Add 1kg sugar, juice of 2 oranges & slug of port. Boil for 8mins. Strain thru gauze & pot.

Preserved Lemons @goodtoweet
Slice 2 lge unwaxed lemons thinly. Dissolve 100g sugar & 25g salt in 300ml water. Boil, reduce heat, add lemons. Poach 10min. Cool. Store in jar.

Lemon Curd @hprw
Juice & zest of 2 lemons, 2 eggs, 175g sugar, 110g butter into bowl on top of a pan of simmering water. Stir till thick. Sterilised jars.

Posh Lemon Curd @simiansuter
28 quail eggs, 3 unwaxed lemons (juice & zest), 300g caster sugar, 200g butter. Cook in a bain-marie until thick.

Dips

Holy Guacamole @hillmelissa
Mash fresh avocados, stir in chopped onions, garlic, tomato, lime juice & lots of chilli!
Melissa Hill, best-selling author of *Something From Tiffany's* & others.

Smokey Guacamole @paulakahumbu
Char2 chillis under grill.Remove skin, chop.Add 2tbsp finely-chopd onion,1 bnch chopd coriander, juice 1lemon, salt.Yum dip 4 fresh carrot!
Paula Kahumbu, ecologist, conservationist & children's author.

Hummus @grumpychit
425g can chickpeas, 1tbsp OO, 2 garlic cloves, 2tbsp lemon juice, 1tsp cumin, 1tbsp tahini. Whiz in blender!

> *@helen_kara*
> Tip: To pass off shop bought hummus as homemade: put in bowl, drizzle EVOO, sprinkle lightly w paprika. Never fails.

Low Fat Hummus *@CountryLets*
1 tin chickpeas, ½ green chilli, ½tsp cumin, 2tbsp lemon juice, 3 cloves minced garlic, 1tbsp chickpea liquid. Blend until smooth.

Chicken-Cheese Dip *@xJennaLeighx*
2 blocks cream cheese, 2 cooked, shredded chicken breasts, 1 pack ranch seasoning, 1 bag pecans. Mix & enjoy!
Jenna Leigh, actress & singer best known for her roles in *Sabrina the Teenage Witch* & onstage in *Wicked*.

Tzatziki *@tcordrey*
Sprinkle grated cucumber w salt. Leave 30 mins. Rinse & pat dry. Mix w plain yogurt, crushed garlic & pepper.

Red Pepper Dip *@CountryLets*
1 red pepper, 1 chilli pepper, 500g cream cheese, 225g sour cream, 1 clove garlic, ½tsp cumin. Blend until smooth. Chill.

Hot Beetroot Dip @CountryLets
250g cooked beetroot (not pickled), 2tbsp hot horseradish sauce, 100ml crème fraîche. Blend until smooth. Season & serve.

Chilli Bean Dip @Tracytid
Tin kidney beans, 70ml sour cream, 2tbsp tomato purée, 2 garlic cloves, ½tsp chilli, 1tsp cumin, 60g grated cheese. Whizz.

Cob Damper Dip @smange
Top& hollow cob loaf. Bake top&insides 200c 10min. Fry bacon,onion,mushrms in buttr. Add red curry paste,flour,milk,sour cream. Put all in loaf.

@smange
Tip: Use the baked inner bread to dip first, then break off bits of the shell as it gets lower.

Raita @PenguinGalaxy
Cut cucumber into very small cubes, stir into plenty of yogurt. Pick loads mint leaves, chop finely, stir in.

Garlic dip @karohemd
Greek yogurt, quark, fresh herbs, crushed garlic, S&P, mustard. Mix & rest in fridge overnight.

Cheese Dip @AndieJ
Boil & soften onions, drain, add milk 2 pan, slowly heat. Add diced cheese, simmer, season. Dunk buttered bread – Yum.

Salsas

Pico De Gallo Salsa @F414
3 onions, 4 tomatoes, 2 jalapeno peppers (all chopped), juice of 2 limes, cilantro, add salt to taste.

Tangy Salsa @janetravers
Finely dice 1 mango, ½ pineapple. Mix together 2cm ginger, grated (inc juice), coriander leaves. Great w fish.

Classic Salsa @angelabdc
Chop together bunch coriander, 1tbsp jalapeños, juice 1 lime in processor. Add punnet cherry plum tomatoes, pulse till chunky.

Chilli Mango Salsa @AbsoluteWrite
Mango, roasted corn, chillis, jalepeño, red onion, tomato, cilantro, garlic, finely chopped. Toss in lime juice w sea salt.

Spice Rubs & Pastes

[L]

Garam masala *@helen_kara*
1tbsp cardamom seeds. 2cm cinnamon stick. 1tsp each cumin seeds, cloves, black peppercorns. 1/3 nutmeg. Grind together.

[L]

New Spice Rub *@tracehillman*
50g each brown sugar & kosher salt, 1tbsp each black pepper, garlic powder, cinnamon, paprika. Taste test tonight!

[L]

Some Like It Hot Curry Powder *@HazelKLarkin*
2tsp each coriander & turmeric; 1tsp each cumin, fenugreek, fennel, amchoor, black pepper; ½tsp each chilli, cinnamon. Mix.

[V]

Harissa *@helen_kara*
Mash garlic, salt, 1tsp coriander seeds, ½tsp cumin seeds, 2-3 red chillis w seeds. Mix w 2tbsp OO to form a paste.

[L] [🕒]

Sweet Tweet Treats

Judging from the many recipes I was sent, the people of Twitter are a sweet-toothed lot. In later chapters you'll find delicious desserts and moreish cakes and bakes, but as I was compiling this book it became abundantly clear that I was going to need a third sweet chapter, to house all those lovely little sweet treats that aren't quite cakes and aren't quite desserts, they're just ... well, they're just because.

Chocolate features strongly in this chapter. Need I say more?

Chocolate!

Gadget Smores @gadgetpolly
2 choc digestives & 3 marshmallows. Mallows on skewer over BBQ, when melting squish between digestives then slide off skewer.
Pollyanna Woodward, British TV presenter currently on *The Gadget Show* on Channel Five

L ⊕ V

Cookie Smores @SusanMallery
Cookie. Dot w minimarshmallows & choc chips. Another cookie. Wrap in foil. Grill for 8 min, flipping once.
Susan Mallery, *New York Times* best-selling romance & women's fiction author.

L

Classic Smores @DazedPuckBunny
A square of chocolate on a graham cracker (digestive biscuit). Flame a marshmallow, blow out, squish between crackers/biccies.

Truffles @bahtocancer
200g dark chocolate, 100ml thick double cream. Melt gently & combine. Leave to thicken then roll lumps in cocoa powder.

Nutty Truffles @CafeFresh
Blend together equal amounts of cocoa powder, nuts, butter & icing sugar – chill 30 mins. Roll & coat w cocoa!

Chocolate Krispie Buns @susiemc1983
Melt some cooking chocolate, add Rice Krispies, spoon chocolate covered krispies into bun cases then set in fridge for 2 hours!
Susan McFadden, musical theatre star (Serena in *Legally Blonde* in the West End), sister of Brian McFadden of Westlife.

Rhino Poo @helen_kara
Destone Medjool dates. Stuff w marzipan. Coat w dark chocolate. Known in our house as 'rhino poo'. Can't remember why.

Chocolate Body Paint @mduffywriter
Heat 150mls cream & 300g choc. Divide 4 pots: 1)drop mint essence 2)drop almond essence 3)shot espresso 4) leave. Paint brush & imagination

Romantic Moments @NettieWriter
Dip strawberries in melted chocolate (dark/milk), leave to dry. Serve w champagne & Nat King Cole playing on the stereo.

My Boy Lollipop @JackyHSF
Melt 225g each milk white & dark choc in microwave. Add chopped nuts/fruit. Pour layers into lightly oiled moulds w sticks. Chill.

Baileys & White Chocolate Fudge @Chiddle84
Heavy pan,stir500g sgr,500ml cream,50ml Baileys, simmer.Boilwhen sgr dissolved.Stir occasionally. Add150g white choc. 22cm LINED tin.Cool.Cut

Chocolate Biscuit Cake @MiriamOCal
2 pkts digestive bisc,55g sugar,115g butter,2tbsp cocoa. Mix crushed biscs in melted butter w sugar & cocoa. Put in tin, cover w meltd choc.

Miriam O'Callaghan, television current affairs broadcaster & chat show host on RTE

Chocolate Biscuit Cake *@JackyHSF*
Melt 300g mlk choc & 25g butter. Bash small pkt Rich Tea biccies, 4 Crunchies & stir in. Press into 15cm sq foil tin. Chill. Cut in squares.

Malteser Squares *@Orbeeque*
Melt 125g butter, 200g chocolate, 75g syrup. Add 150g crushed biscuits & as many Maltesers as you like. Press mix into loaf tin, cool.

Fruity Chocolate Biscuit Cake *@Lyvit*
Melt 200g chocolate, 2tbsp syrup, 125g butter in a bowl; add 200g crushed digestives, some almonds, cherries, raisins. Set in a dish.

Crispy Mars Bar Slices *@mduffywriter*
Melt 80g butter, 1tbsp golden syrup, 4 Mars bars. Stir in 3 cups Rice Krispies & cup raisins. Press into tray. Fridge. Slice.

Fridge Bars *@chiddle84*
Heat 85g butter,4tbsp golden syrup.Melt 200gdark choc. Mix.Add 1 egg.Whisk.Add 50g walnuts,sultanas,cherries. 100gdigestive bisc.Fridge 12hrs

Crunchy Bars *@mduffywriter*
[L]
Melt 300g choc, 100g butter, 3tbsp golden syrup. Add broken Crunchie, ginger biscuits, Maltesers, nuts, raisins. Tray, fridge, slice.

[V]

Tiffin *@MrsCordial*
[L]
Melt 170g butter, 4tbsp syrup, 280g choc. Then add raisins, broken biscuits, cherries, dates. Chill. Top w layer melted choc. Chill.

[V]

Chewy Marshmallow Squares *@thejayfaulkner*
[L]
Melt 510g choc & 414ml condensed milk. Stir in 2tbsp butter, 1½tsp vanilla extract, mini-marshmallows. Spread in lined pan. Chill & cut.

[V]

Mellow Mallow Mammy *@mduffywriter*
Melt bowl of chocolate (don't let kids see!) Place large marshmallow on each fingertip. Find quiet corner & dip, lick, suck & bite. Mmm!

[L]

Haystacks *@JackyHSF*
[L]
Melt 4 parts dark, 1 part milk choc chips. Mix in 2 parts chopped nuts, 2 parts noodles or bran. Drop teaspoons onto baking paper. Chill.

[V]

Not So Much Chocolate – But Still Good!

Hazelnut Brittle @jollyolly
Heat 300g caster sugar, add 100g skinned, chopped hazelnuts, tip onto baking paper, snap & serve after 20 min.

Olly Smith, Presenter of *Iron Chef UK*, regular on BBC1's *Saturday Kitchen*, columnist for *The Mail on Sunday's Live Magazine*. Author of *'Eat & Drink'*.

[L] [V]

Crunchy Mallow Squares @Chiddle84
Melt 2 bags marshmallows w 85g butter. Crush Crunchies, add to mix. Pour in Rice Crispies as needed. Baking tray. Set.

[V]

Chewy Granola Bars @CountryLets
Melt 2 bags marshmallows, 85g butter in pan. Stir in granola, raisins, rice cereal, nuts. Press into oiled tin. Cool. Cut into bars.

[V]

Crunch @davidgilray
Large pan, 1tbsp water, 4tbsp syrup, 200g sugar. Simmer 5-10mins. Mix in 3tsp sodium bicarbonate. Into greased tin, cool, break in chunks.

[L]

Crunch 2, Return Of The Crunch
@davidgilray

Melt choc & dip chunks of crunch. Or melt choc, add crunch bits, raisins, Rice Krispies & spoon into cake cases.

Peanut Butter Bars *@Donna_Tilling*

Mix 50g muscovado sugar, 200g icing sugar, 50g butter, 200g peanut butter. Put in shallow tray. Melt 300g choc & pour over. Set in fridge.

Dates With Sweet Cheese *@helen_kara*

Destone Medjool dates. Stuff w dolcelatte.

Crispy Peanut Butter Squares *@JackyHSF*

Melt 8tbsp peanut butter, 8tbsp butter, 4tbsp honey. Add 110g Rice Krispies, 190g chopped apricot. Press in 22x33cm pan. Chill. Cut bars.

Easy After Dinner Mints *@mduffywriter*

Whisk eggwhite till stiff. Add 350g icing sug, 3 drops mint ess, 2 drops green colour. Roll tsp size & flatten on tray w fork. Cool 1hr.

@mduffywriter
To make the previous *Tweet Treats* sweets even yummier, dip in melted choc when cool for mint choc sweets.

Golden Biscuit Cake *@Tracytid*
Melt 125g butter, 3tbsp golden syrup, bash 200g biscuits, mix together, put in tray in fridge for couple of hrs. Eat.

V

Simple Syrup *@janetravers*
In a saucepan combine equal volumes sugar & water. Bring to boil, stirring, until sugar has dissolved. Allow to cool. Useful for many recipes.

Desserts

'Save room for dessert' – it's what we all say, isn't it? Well, I've certainly saved room for dessert in this book, as I received more recipes for desserts and cakes than for any other category. As a result, this is the most jam-packed chapter.

Our celebrities are also fond of their treats. You'll find nineteen celebrities featured in this chapter alone.

You might find the classifications in this chapter unusual.

The topic led to lengthy debates on Twitter, as we discussed the different meanings of 'tart' vs 'pie' depending on whether you're English or Irish. Sparks flew over the question of whether pavlova and cheesecake count as tarts (the consensus was that they don't), and don't get me started on the subject of crumble!

In the end, I decided to classify desserts in a way that makes sense to me. I hope it makes sense to you, too.

Ice-Cream, Frozen Desserts & Toppings

Boozy Ice-Cream Sundae @janjonesauthor
Tall glass. Slurp of ouzo. Slurp of advocaat. Spoon in vanilla ice cream to fill. Top up w fizzy lemon & stir. Delicious!

Jan Jones, award-winning author of Regency romance and contemporary romantic comedy.

Crunchie Ice-Cream @mduffywriter
Whisk 570ml dbl cream. Fold in tin condensed milk. Chop 3 Crunchie Bars & add to mix. Put in container. Freeze for yummy ice-cream.

Mango Ice-Cream @MJulieMiller
Caramelise 400g tin evaporated milk, then beat till double. Add 175g lemon juice, 175g icing sugar, 800g tinned mango purée. Mix. Freeze.

V

Marshmallow Ice-Cream @mduffywriter
Heat 140ml cream & 170g marshmallows till melted. Cool. Whip 280ml double cream & fold in to mix. Freeze.

Rose Ice-Cream @asgerd
Beat3 yolks,60g sugar.Add 200ml hot milk,return to pan. Heat.Chill,add3tbsp rosewater,vanilla,150ml cream,drop red colour.Freeze,beat,freeze.

The Candy Man Can @DazedPuckBunny
Chop Dime, Snickers & Milky Way bars into softened vanilla ice cream, re-freeze until set. Serve w caramel sauce.

L

Brown Cow Ice-Cream Soda @JanetRudolph
Put rootbeer in glass, leave 5cm. Drop in chocolate ice cream. Drizzle chocolate syrup on top.
Janet Rudolph, crime fiction writer and chocolate lover.

Melon Sorbet @MontanaGael
1 honeydew melon, 250ml simple syrup, juice 1 lemon. Blend, then freeze in metal pan. Cool on tongue!

For simple syrup see page 146

Gin & Tonic Sorbet @rosamundi
Heat 28ml tonic & 25g sugar till sugar dissolves. Cool. Stir in 140ml gin. Freeze in rigid container 3hrs. Stir. Freeze overnight.

Rhubarb Ice @Gargarin
1 tin condensed milk, same amount cooked sweetened rhubarb: freeze & stir. Serves 2-4 people. Preparation time: 3hrs.

Frozen Banana Mousse @NotEvsie
Freeze a banana, peel & blend to the consistency of a mousse. Add honey &/or cinnamon to taste - delicious, natural, quick.

The Easily-Pleased Dessert
@realkaywoodward
Find clotted cream ice cream in freezer. Hurray! 2 scoops each. Now chocolate powder (top shelf of cupboard). Sprinkle on LOADS.

Kay Woodward, author of *Jane Airhead* and the *Skate School* series.

Ryan's Ready Treat @TubridyTweets
Ok, take one slice of HB ice cream, two fresh wafers & nothing else. Place ice cream between the wafers. Et voila! ;)

Ryan Tubridy, Irish radio and television personality, host of *The Late Late Show*.

The Frozen Monkey @ElizabethBastos
Banana: slice and fill with peanut butter, dip in melted chocolate, then freeze.

Toppings

Peanut Butter Sauce @JillMansell
Equal amounts of hard butter and peanut butter, melt in microwave for 30 secs, add pinch of salt then pour over vanilla ice cream. It sets!

Jill Mansell, best-selling author whose books have sold over 3 million copies.

Easiest Fudge Sauce @annerooney
Put fudge & a small amount of milk in a jug and microwave till gooey. Stir till fudge melted. Pour over vanilla ice cream. Mmm.

Fab Choccie Sauce @KatieFforde
Equal amounts butter, golden syrup, cocoa powder (say 1tbsp each). Melt in pan low heat. If too strong add a little cream.
Katie Fforde, best-selling romance novelist and president of the Romantic Novelist's Association.

Gooey Mars Bar Sauce @mduffywriter
Boil 140ml double cream. Add 2 chopped Mars Bars & 50g choc. Lid on & turn off heat. When choc melts stir & pour on ice-cream. Yum.

Toffee Sauce @SCallejo
Infuse cardamom, vanilla pod in 240ml single cream. Add to syrup of 100g sugar melted w 30ml water. Simmer until dense.

Strawberry Sauce @goodtoweet
Blitz 150g fresh strawberries w 1tbsp icing sugar & a squeeze of orange juice. Chill and serve over ice-cream or swirl through yogurt.

Funky Monkey Banana Sauce @aurora111
Melt 50g butter in pan. Add 150g brown sugar till dissolved. Add 4 sliced bananas till caramelised. Stir in 50ml cream. Spoon over ice-cream.

Easy Fruit Desserts – Some No-Cook!

Pineapple With Cointreau @LoreleiKing
Quarter a pineapple longways. Segment each 'boat'. Drizzle each boat w 1tbsp of Cointreau. Gorgeous & good for the voice!
Lorelei King, Actress (*Cold Feet, Notting Hill, Emmerdale, Chef*), audiobook narrator, voiceover artist, writer.

Fruit Fondue @helen_kara
Melt dark choc, dip toothsome fruits (satsuma segments, strawberries, grapes, cherries etc) & everyone will be your friend.

Apricots In Brandy @christinemosler
Chop dried apricots, soak in brandy and honey for 2 hours (less if you can't wait). Serve w crème fraîche.

Easy Pear Pie @inkwellHQ
Crush choc chip cookies & soak in sherry overnight. Add layer chopped tinned pears then layer of whipped cream.

Best Baked Apples @mduffywriter
Peel & core 4 apples. Slice 2 Mars Bars. Stuff apples w Mars Bars & cover with foil. Bake 160c 30mins. Serve w ice-cream.

Grilled Pineapple @janetravers
Thick slices fresh pineapple, generous brown sugar all over. Grill each side till sugar caramelises. Serve w fresh cream/yogurt.

Four Ways With Bananas

@Gillian_Phillip
Halve a banana, sprinkle over brown sugar & douse with rum. Wrap in tinfoil, bake 10 mins.
Gillian Phillip, acclaimed author of *Firebrand* and *The Opposite of Amber* plus many others.

@helen_kara
Halve 4 bananas lengthwise, add slosh of Calvados, squeeze fresh lemon, sprinkle muscovado sugar, knob butter. 160c 20 mins.

@CLButler76
Peel & cut along a banana. Put choccy buttons into the cut, wrap in foil & bake in BBQ/fire embers.

@hmhunt
Thread sprig of rosemary through unpeeled banana. Wrap in foil. Bake or cook on barbecue. Split open & add ice-cream.

Baked Figs @SparkleyTwinkle
Fresh figs, cut cross in top & insert good dark choc. Wrap in foil, BBQ till warm. Open foil, spoon of double cream in top. Yum!

Fruit Kebabs @cathryanhoward
Skewer banana pieces, strawberries & kiwis. Brush lightly w melted butter & lemon juice. Grill. YUM.

Cheesecake, Pavlova & Cold Desserts

Lemon Cheesecake @MrsAggers
Crushed biscuit base. Mix tin condensed milk, same amount of double cream & juice of 3 lemons and pour over base. Chill & scoff!

Emma Agnew, journalist and wife of cricket commentator Jonathon 'Aggers' Agnew.

Easy Cheesecake @mduffywriter
Base: Crush digestives in melt butter. Top: Dissolve jelly in 140ml boil water. Whisk in pkt cream cheese, 140ml cream, natural yogurt. Fridge.

@mduffywriter
Tips for aforementioned cheesecake: use lime jelly & lemon juice for lemon & lime flavour, or strawberry jelly & chopped strawberries for strawberry cheesecake.

Cheat's Cheesecake @keris
Mascarpone cheese & ginger biscuit = tiny cheesecake (you can add half a strawberry, if you want to be 'healthy')
Keris Stainton, author of *Della Says: OMG!*

Pavlova @EnglishMum
Whip4 egg whites to soft peaks, add 225g sugar slowly till glossy. Circle on baking tray. 150c 40mins. Cool. Soft whipped cream&ripe fruits.

Chocolate Pavlova @janetravers
Melt 200g 70% choc, cool slightly, fold into whipped cream. Pour onto large Pavlova case, top w raspberries.

Eton Mess @DebbieRush1
Big bowl, crushed up chewy gooey meringues, handful of strawberries and blackberries w huge pile of fresh double cream poured over! Heaven!!
Debbie Rush, actress best known for her role as Anna Windass in *Coronation Street*.

Chocolate Lime Cups @mduffywriter
Heat 50g sugar, juice of 1 lime, 1tbsp water till sugar melts. Cool. Add 300ml cream. Whisk to peak. Stir in 85g grated choc. Chill in cups.

TWEET TREATS

Raspberry Fool @CountryLets
Whip up some double cream w sugar. Crush raspberries & stir into the cream, saving some raspberries for topping. Serve w biscuits.

Strawberry & Elderflower Jelly @LadyBirdFi
Dissolve 4 soft gelatine leaves in 450ml boiling water. Add 150ml elderflower cordial, stir, pour over 350g diced ripe strawbs. Leave to set.
Fi Bird, author of *Kids' Kitchen*.

Boozy Prunes @VEE6
Soak stoned prunes in whisky & tea for 1hr, then drain. Chill, melt chocolate over, serve w cream.

Bueno Berries @Soriko
Lightly mash up a bar of Kinder Bueno white & mix w some fresh strawberries (halved) ...Voila, delicious!

Sweet Soup @helen_kara
Blend red summer fruits w yogurt/single cream, add sugar or honey if necessary. Serve w shortbread or tuiles.

Perfect Digestif @mikelcu
Ice-cold fairtrade 90% cocao chocolate. Laphroaig. Remind your taste buds (& dentist) why they are there....

Puddings

Crème Brûlée @justinbrownchef
Whisk 5 egg yolks, 113g caster sugar. Heat 570ml double cream, seeds of 1 vanilla pod. Mix. Into ramekins/small dishes, bake 140c 40mins.

Justin Brown, Chef of the year 2009/2010, Food writer, BBC2 *Masterchef*, Jamie Oliver Happy Days tour, BBC Radio, restaurant owner.

Creamy Rice Pudding @HelenRedders
100g short grain rice, 50g sugar, 1.1litres full fat milk. Lots of grated nutmeg. Low oven for 2 hours.

Greek Rice Pudding @MJulieMiller
Hob: 170g pud rice, lemn zest, 1.1litres milk till soft.Add 170g sugar,2tsp cornflr mixed 2 paste w milk.Cook till creamy.Cinnamon.Chill.

Spotted Dick @rebeccaebrown
1 part flour, 1 part sugar, 0.5 part suet, glug orange juice & jar sweet mincemeat. Mix, microwave 5 mins.

Spanish Bread Pudding @SCallejo
Sliced bread in deep dish. Pour on milk infused w sugar,vanilla extract,cinnamon stick. Rest 24h. Sprinkle sugar, burn w torch.

Bierko's Bad Pudding @MrCraigBierko
Sugar, Milk, Cacao, Salmon, Thumb Tacks, Hand, Dorm Bathroom Sponge, Pudding.
Craig Bierko, Award-winning American actor best known for his roles in *The Long Kiss Goodnight* and *Scary Movie 4*

Lower Fat Bread & Butter Pudding @janetravers
In oiled dish:bread w low-fat spread,scatter sultanas. Beat2eggs,500ml milk,1tbsp crème fraîche, pour over. Nutmeg.Rest 30mins.160c 20-30mins.

Capirotada: Mexican Bread Pudding @DazedPuckBunny
Boil cinnamon sticks & 300g brwn sugar. Pour resulting syrup over bread in dish. Add raisins, cheddar cheese, apple cubes. Bake 180c 20mins.

Summer Pudding @NaughtyPusPuss
Line small pyrex bowl w sponge fingers. Fill w raspberries and blueberries. Cover all w jelly, leave to set. Turn onto plate. Yummy...

Choc Fudgy Pud @PenguinGalaxy
Cake mix into greased pie dish. Pour on 190ml boiling water, 56g brown sugar, 56g cocoa. Bake, sauce will sink.

Chocolate Mousse @sarasheridan
Whiz two bars 70% dark choc. Add 15 cardamom seeds, tub double cream (heated) and an egg. Fridge. Best mousse ever.

Sara Sheridan, best-selling writer of The Secret of the Sands and others.

Boozy Ginger Pineapple @Gillian_Phillip
Pour rum & Crabbies ginger wine over sliced pineapple. Sprinkle w sugar & grill.

Gillian Phillip, acclaimed author of Firebrand and The Opposite of Amber plus many others.

Crumbles & Hot Desserts

Cthulhu Crumble @neilhimself
Top: 120g oat flour, 135g brown sugar, 2tbsp crushed nuts, 115g butter, 1tsp salt. Under: sour cherries. Bake 190c 45mins.

Neil Gaiman, author of American Gods & The Graveyard Book, winner of multiple awards including the Carnegie Medal, 3 Hugos, 2 Nebulas, 1 World Fantasy Award, 4 Bram Stoker Awards & many more.

Amaretti Peach Crumble @maggiephilbin
Halve and stone peaches. Crumble Amaretti biscuits & lemon juice on top. Roast in oven 180c 20mins. Serve w ice cream.

Maggie Philbin, BBC journalist specialising in technology — *Tomorrow's World*!

L 🕐 **V**

Best Ever Crumble @helen_kara
60g each rolled oats & flaked almonds.85g each brown flour, muscovado sugar, butter.Melt butter, mix in rest. Bake on filling of your choice.

V

Poached Pears @goodtoweet
Poach peeled pear in 150ml red wine, 100g sugar & orange zest, till soft c.30mins.Remove pear, boil liquid – reduce to syrup.Pour over pear.

L

Poire Belle Hélène @PottiJo
Hot poached pears, hot chocolate sauce and ice cream. Enjoy!

Roast Rhubarb @goodtoweet
Roast 6cm sticks of rhubarb, sprinkled liberally w vanilla sugar & splash white wine 180c 20-30mins, till tender. Serve warm with cream.

V

Hot Mango Sauce @PeterGreste
Melt butter. Toss in nearly-ripe mango pieces. Add 1 lime, rind & juice. Sugar to taste. Serve hot w pancakes.
Peter Greste, Africa newshound, snapper and broadcaster.

L

Flambéed Pineapple @SanyaV
Fry slices of pineapple in butter, flambé w tequila. Serve w coconut ice-cream. Drizzle melted dark chocolate on top.

V 🕐

Pies & Tarts

Medieval Marchpane Pie @Chadwickauthor
Fill cooked pastry case w stewed apple. Dot w bits of marzipan, cook in mod hot oven till marzipan rich brown & sort of crispy on top.
Elizabeth Chadwick, award-winning, best-selling author of historical fiction including *To Defy a King* & *Lady of the English*.

L **V**

Bramble Tart @JackyHSF
Fill pastry disc w breadcrumbs, wedges of apple and blackberries. Sprinkle sugar & lemon zest. Fold edges over. Bake 180c 35 mins.

V

Easy Apple Turnover Pie @CountryLets
Melt butter & sugar in ovenproof pan. Add sliced apple, top with puff pastry. Brush egg, bake 200c 20 min, tip out on plate.

Almond-Apple Pie @honeysock
1can almond pie filling,3sliced apples in pastry case.Top 100g digestive bisc crumbs, 100g sliced almonds.Bake 180c 35 min til gold&crunchy.

Blueberry Tart @chiddle84
Line tin w pastry.Mix50g sugar,20g flour,325g blueberries.In pastry case.Oven 220c 15mins then180c 30mins more.Remove.325g more blueberries.

Rhubarb & Strawberry Open Tarts @JackyHSF
Mix rhubarb chunks, halved strawberries, sugar, little flour.Put blobs in centre of 18cm circles pastry.Fold in edges. Chill. 180c 25mins.

Custard Tart @chiddle84
Blind bake pastry case. Heat 750ml cream. Whisk 12 egg yolks,115g caster sugar & the cream. Into pastry case, shake allspice. 200c 50mins.

Cakes & Bakes

Ah, cake! The smell of home-baking, those delicious aromas of sugar, vanilla and chocolate wafting from the kitchen; the texture of freshly-baked sponge melting in the mouth, cream oozing from between the layers ... And biscuits, the snap, the crumble, the dunk in your tea. The moreishness of it all!

Who doesn't love home baking? It doesn't have to be an elaborate ritual, reserved only for special occasions and dreaded for weeks in advance. With the following recipes you can throw together delectable baked goods, most of which can be prepared in minutes. Want to know how to win friends and influence people? The answer is in this chapter!

For some of the bread recipes a breadmaker is required, but most can be baked directly in the oven and are surprisingly simple to make. As stated before, where a recipe reads 'flour' it refers to plain flour while 'SR flour' is self-raising. Happy baking!

Cakes

Algernon's Solution @MrUku

Recipes? Here's one, buy cake. Serve. It's all my own work. I expect a front page credit.

Chocolate Courgette Cake @ConorWilson
Mix:175g mltd dk choc,200g flour,1tsp bak pwder,1tsp bicarb,225g grated courgette,1tsp cinnamon,110g caster sugar,2eggs,175ml oil.180c 1 hr.

For chocolate butter icing see page 166

Moist Carrot Cake @jancyoverell
Mix 360g flour, 2tsp bak pwder, 2tsp cinnamon, 350ml oil, 2tsp vanilla,400g sugar, 270g grated carrot,can pineapple,3eggs.Bake 180c 45+mins.

Olive Oil Cake @CountryLets
Beat 5eggs.Add 150gcaster sug,whisk til mix 3 times bigger.Add50ml OO by drops while beating.Sift,fold 150gflour.160c 40-45mins.Icing sugr.

Lemon Cake @goodtoweet
Beat 200g each butter & sugar till pale. Whisk in 2 eggs, 600g SR flour & zest 1 lemon. Bake 180c 40mins+. Try warm w cream.

Easy Coffee Walnut Cake @JosaYoung
250g each butter& sugar,4 eggs,300g SR flour.Whizz together, add2 handful walnuts.Bake lined tin 180c 30mins.Sandwich w coffee butter cream.

Chocolate Cake @PintAndAHaircut
[L] Sieve 120g SR flour, add 200g sugar, 190ml milk, 165g melted butter, 2 eggs, 2tbsp cocoa, ½tsp baking powder. Whisk,greased tin 180c 20mins. **[V]**

Chocolate Fudge Cake @RosemaryMacCabe
[L] Melt 113g butter, add 284g sugar. Take off heat, add 2 eggs. Mix well, add 170g flour & 56g drinking choc/cocoa. 30cm tin, 180c 40mins. **[V]**

Flourless Chocolate Cake @TheLibraryGal
[L] Melt200gr drk choc,1tsp watr low heat.Add100gr butter slowly.Off heat,slowly add100g sugr,1tsp cornflr,4egg yolks&whiskd whites.180c 25mins. **[V]**

Eleanor Pringle's Ginger Torte @davidgilray
[V] 56g caster sugr,113g buttr,170g flour,56g crushd digestvs. Make 2 rounds.120c 50min.Sandwich w butter icing&ground ginger.Top w glacé icing.

Gâteau Breton @SanyaV
[L] 225g plain flour,250g sugar,250g butter (cubed),6 egg yolks.Mix.Tin.Glaze w 1tsp yolk,1tbsp water.Bake 190c 15mins then 180c 25 mins more. **[V]**

Apple Cake @goodtoweet
Whisk 200g each butter & sugar till pale. Whisk in 2eggs & 600g SR flour. Stir in 1 diced apple. Bake in flat tin, 180c till golden.

White Chocolate & Raspberry Brownies @carolwhead
250g white choc,75g butter,125g sugr,2 eggs,1tsp vanilla,150g flour,½tsp salt,150g raspberries. Melt 175g choc, stir in all.180c 30 mins.

Toppings & Fillings

Best Chocolate Icing Ever @helen_kara
200g 70% dark choc, 50g unsalted butter. Melt & mix, spread on cake. Leave to cool if you have the willpower!

Easy Chocolate Icing @dorristheloris
Stir 200g chopped galaxy bar into an equal quantity of near-boiling double cream. Mix & pour over choc cake for easy icing!

Chocolate Butter Icing @ConorWilson
350g icing sugar & 50g cocoa powder sifted into 175g creamed butter. Beat. Drop of water or liqueur, optional. Perfect w choc courgette cake!

Boozy Cream Cake Filling @PenguinGalaxy
[L] Whip 150ml cream. Dissolve 1tsp instant coffee (or 1 shot espresso) in 50ml Tia Maria. Fold into cream w 100g grated dark chocolate.

Buns, Muffins & Individual Cakes

Madeleines For Tea? @TrishDeseine
Whisk 3 eggs&130g sugar to white & fluffy. Add 125g melted butter, 150g flour, zest 1 lemon, ½tsp bak pwdr. Grease madeleine tin. 220c 5-7 mins.

Trish Deseine, Irish food/recipe writer for French *ELLE, ELLE à Table*, cookbook author.

Basic Buns @enormous
[L] Cream together 125g each SR flour, butter, caster sugar w 2 eggs, 1tsp vanilla essence. Whisk till smooth. In lined cases 180c 15 mins.

White Chocolate & Raspberry Buns @Lauraann1061
[L] Mix 200g each SR flour, caster sugar, butter. Add 4eggs, 1tsp vanilla, 75g white choc. Into cases, add 2 raspberries each. 160c 15 mins.

Maple Walnut Cupcakes *@chiddle84*
Make basic cupcake recipe. Add 50g chopped walnuts, 4tbsp maple syrup. Bake 12 mins. Mix cream cheese,sugar,maple syrup,butter for icing.

For basic buns see page 167

Chocolate Treasure Cakes *@Lyvit*
2 eggs, 100g flour, 100g sugar, 100g butter, 2 packets chocolate M&Ms. Mix together & bake in cases 180c 15-18 mins.

Banana Buns *@chiddle84*
Cream 125g butter,125g caster sugar.Beat in 2 eggs till smooth.Fold in 125g flour,2tsp bak powder, 2 mashed'nanas.Bun cases. 180c 20mins.

Welshcakes *@beth_tk*
225g SR flour, 113g butter, 28g sugar, 1 egg, 1tbsp milk, sultanas. Mix into biscuit shapes then griddle to golden brown.

Muffins *@goodtoweet*
Mix 150g SR flour, 1tsp cinnamon, 50g sugar, 1egg, 50ml each milk & sunflower oil. Add 100g berries. Bake in muffin tin 180c 20mins.

Muffin In A Mug @JackyHSF
Put 4tbsp each SR flour & sugar, 2tbsp cocoa, 1 egg, 3tbsp each milk & oil, ½tsp coffee essence in large mug. Microwave 3 mins@max. Tip out.

[L][V]

Biscuits & Cookies

Rachel Allen's Easiest Cookies @RachAllen1
Mix 56g caster sugar, 112g soft butter & 170g flour. Roll 5mm thick, cut into shapes. Bake 180c till light golden.
Rachel Allen, best-selling cookbook author and cookery programme presenter.

[L][⏲][V]

Anzac Biscuits @bradatslice
Mix 75g butter, 80g coconut, 90g oats, 125g flour, 200g sugar w 3tbsp golden syrup & splash warm water. Roll balls, on tray. 175c 15-20mins.

[V]

Golden Syrup Cookies @chiddle84
Cream 115g butter w 100g sugar. Add 1tbsp golden syrup, ½tsp vanilla, pinch salt, 120g SR flour. Form balls, bake 170c 12 mins.

[V]

Peanut Butter Cookies @RFLong
260g peanut butter, 100g white sugar, 1 egg. Mix to paste. 12 blobs on baking tray (they spread). 160c 10-15 mins. Crisp, chewy when cool.
Ruth Long, Writer of fantasy & paranormal romance inc *The Scroll Thief* & *The Wolf's Sister*.

[⏲][L][V]

TWEET TREATS

Orange Biscuits *@goodtoweet*
Mix 225g butter, 110g sugar, 300g SR flour, zest 1orange to form dough. Flatten small balls w fork on baking sheet. 180c 8-9 mins.

L

Cardamom Orange Cookies *@nosycrow*
Mix 28g ground rice, 56g caster sugar, 113g flour, 113g butter, cardamom & orange zest to dough. Chill. Cut shapes. 175c 15 mins.

V

Sugar Candy Kisses *@JackyHSF*
Cream225g buttr,100g ic.sugar,1tsp vanilla,270g flour,¼tsp salt,120g chpd nuts.Chill.Form 3cm balls round Hershey choc kisses.200c 8-12 min.

Irish Oatmeal Cookies *@janetravers*
Combine 125g soft butter,50g caster sugar,150g flour,50g oatmeal,1tsp vanilla. Roll walnut-size balls, flatten top w fork, bake 180c 15 min.

V

Chewy Oatmeal Cookies *@SelenaGovier*
Mix 75g each plain flour, oatmeal, brown sugar, 1tsp bicarb. Melt 75g butter,1tbsp gol syrup. Mix wet w dry. Baking sheet, 170c 12mins.

V

Almond Cookies @mduffywriter
Mix 113g ground almonds, 113g sugar, 4 drops almond essence. Bind w egg yolk. Knead & form balls. Flatten. Almond on top each. 180c 10 mins.

Almond Ginger Macaroons @queenofpots
Whisk 1eggwhte to stiff. Whisk in 100g light br.sugar. Fold in 100g grnd almond, 1tsp grnd ginger. Spoon on lined baking sheet. 180c 20 mins.

Shortbread @JoannaSchaff
225g each flour & melted butter,113g each sugar & cornflour.Mix.Press dough into round, prick surface, score wedge lines. Bake gold 150c.

Basic Flapjacks @clairecatrina
Melt 100g butter,125g caster sugar together.Add 1tbsp golden syrup,175g oats, stir. Press in greased tin, bake175c 25 mins.Cool, cut, serve.

Fruity Flapjacks @mduffywriter
Heat 175g butter,125g brown sugar,55g gold syrup. Add 350g oats, 60g raisins, 60gsunflower seeds. Bake on tray 180c 30 mins. Cut in squares.

Bread

Soda Bread @goodtoweet
Sieve 450g white flour, 1tsp bicarb soda, 1tsp salt. Form dough w 450ml soured milk. Knead, round, flatten, bake 200c 40mins.

Brown Soda Bread @mduffywriter
Mix 400g each white & wholemeal flour, 1tsp bread soda & salt. Mix 570ml buttermilk. Knead, form round. 200c 45 mins. Cool.

Cheese & Chive Soda Bread @mduffywriter
Mix 250g flour, pnch salt, 1tbsp bread soda. Rub in 20g butter. Add 1egg, 175g buttermilk, 75g cheese, 15g chives. Tin. Oven 200c 40mins.

@JoannaSchaff
Tip: Soda bread is ready when you tap the base & it makes a hollow knocking sound.

Olive Oil Bread @karenquah
Mix 500g plain flour, 8g yeast, 1tsp each sugar & salt, 5tbsp OO. Add 300ml warm water. Knead. Leave 30mins. Bake 200c 40mins.

Olive & Garlic Bread @HazelKLarkin
225g black olives,300ml water,1½tbsp butter, 1½tbsp brown sugar, 5 clvs garlic, 400g bread flour, 2¼tsp yeast. In bread machine press start!

V

Scones @RFLong
Sift 105g flour,2tsp sugar,pinch salt,1½tsp baking powder.Rub in 30g marg,5tbsp milk to soft dough.Roll to 5 mm, cut 6 rounds. 220c 12 mins.

Ruth Long, writer of fantasy & paranormal romance inc *The Scroll Thief* & *The Wolf's Sister*.

V

Brioche @Danoosha
Stir 3tbsp milk into 60g melted butter.Add 2 eggs,30g sugar,275g flour,1 sachet yeast,1tsp mix spice. Set breadmaker: sweet 500g loaf.

V

Banana Bread @thornae
Mash 4 v. ripe bananas w 76g butter. Add 200g sugar,1 egg,1tsp vanilla,1tsp baking soda,pinch salt. Mix, 340g flour. Bake 180c 1 hour.

V

Banana Nut Bread @mduffywriter
Fold: 225g flour, 1tsp each salt,baking powder,cinnamon. Add 115g sugar,1 egg,110ml sunfl oil,57g pecans,4 mashed bananas.Loaf tin.180c 1 hr.

V

Border Tart @davidgilray
Cream 2tbsp butter, 150g demerara sugar. Add 1egg, 150g mixed fruit, 1dsp SR flour. Into shortcrust pastry case. Bake 180c till brown.

V

Gypsy Tart @Lawraah
Whisk 400g evaporated milk w 350g muscovado sugar. Pour into 25cm pastry case & bake 200c 10mins.

L V

Cheat's Tarte Tatin @NettieWriter
Roll out puff pastry. Arrange apple slices & sultanas on top. Sprinkle w brown sugar & cinnamon. 180c 20-30mins or till golden.

L V

Apple Puff Pastry Squares @JackyHSF
Cut 375g puff pastry into 8, overlap apple slices on top, sprinkle w sugar, bake 180c 20mins. Spread w apricot glaze while warm.

L

Pineapple Pie Filling @DazedPuckBunny
4eggs, 500ml milk, 2tbsp butter, salt, 1canpineapple w juice, 6tbsp flour, 450g sugar. Simmer till filling thickens. Bake in pastry case.

V

Coconut Pie *@thejayfaulkner*
Mix 50g butter, 50g sugar, 100g coconut, 1 egg. Shortcrust pastry in pie tin. Add strawberry jam, fill w coconut mixture. Cook 190c 15mins.

V

Key Lime Pie *@thejoyoffood*
180ml lime juice, 2 cans sweetened condensed milk, 250ml sour cream. Mix well, pour into pastry case. 180c 10-15 mins then chill. Cream.

L V

Banoffee Pie *@CountryLets*
Top a ready-made sweet shortcrust pastry base w a jar of caramel, sliced bananas, whipped double cream and grated chocolate.

L V

Party Food

• • • • • • • • • • • • • •

If, like me, your hosting skills stretch to a few packets of dry roasted peanuts and some frozen cocktail sausages, then read on. Once you've tried to roast your own, you'll never go back to packets of stale, dusty nuts again!

There are recipes in the following chapter for easy cold canapés, casual grab-a-loaf-and-dig-in baked cheeses, and sweet and savoury nibbles of all kinds. Combine the following recipes with a few of the dips from the 'Spreads, Dips & Preserves' chapter and your next party will be one to remember. Actually, why not throw a party just to try these recipes out? It's as good an excuse as any!

Nuts & Nibbles

Spicy Toasted Nuts @beecee
Toast pecans or mixed nuts w chilli, Tabasco, salt & oil. Hot oven till browned.

Tamari Nuts @helen_kara
Sauté 360g mixed nuts in 2tsp oil till gold. Mix tog 1tbsp tamari, ¼tsp cayenne, squeeze lemon juice. Add to nuts, mix well.

Sweet & Salty Rosemary Nuts @SanyaV
Oven-toast assorted nuts. Mix chopped fresh rosemary, muscovado sugar, salt, cayenne pepper, melted unsalted butter. Mix w nuts.

Chilli Almonds @goodtoweet
Heat 2tsp EVOO in heavy pan. Add 255g peeled almonds. Fry till golden brown. Add 3 ground, dried chillies & plenty sea salt. Serve w drinks.

Baked Seeds *@NETNSparents*
Mix equal quantities of sunflower & pumpkin seeds. Coat liberally in soy sauce. Bake 5 mins hot oven.

Caramel Popcorn *@HelenRedders*
50g popping corn. Microwave 2.5 mins x 4. Melt 140g butter & muscovado sugar till dissolved. Pour over popcorn.

Crunchy Chickpeas *@RhondaParrish*
Open can of chickpeas. Rinse. Spread on cookie sheet & drizzle w OO. Season w curry powder or seasoning salt. Bake 180c till crisp.

Parsnip Crisps *@FutureNostalgic*
Thinly slice parsnips, deep fry till crispy, sprinkle w salt & enjoy homemade parsnip crisps. Gorgeous w a hint of sweetness.

Courgette Crisps *@JoannaSchaff*
Thinly slice courgettes, brush w OO. Fry or grill, about 2 mins per side. Sprinkle w salt. Serve alone or as side.

Amazing Cracker Snack *@honeysock*
Soak saltine crackers in water just to bloat. Brush 2 sides w melted butter & cayenne pepper. Bake 200c until crispy.

Wholegrain Triangles @jennyfoxe
Roll out some slices of wholegrain bread till flat. Cut into small triangles, brush w OO. Bake medium oven for 20mins. Salt.

Sweet Cinnamon Chips'N'Dip @JackyHSF
Cut sheets fresh lasagne into triangles. Deep fry till gold. Drain. Dip in mixed caster sugar & cinnamon. Serve w whipped cream to dip.

Sweet Amaretto Dip @mduffywriter
Heat 140ml dbl cream & 280g choc in pot. Stir in 3tbsp amaretto liqueur. Dip strawberries in for a taste sensation!

Marinated Watermelon @raingraves
Cut watermelon into chunks. Add chopped fresh basil. Soak in Moscato wine or vodka; serve chilled.

Savoury Marinated Watermelon @raingraves
Cut watermelon into chunks as above, then sprinkle a little sea salt & cracked black pepper for a more savoury flavour:)

Hot & Cold Canapés

Jellied Bloody Mary *@brit_battleaxe*
Make greatest Bloody Mary you can, add gelatine. Pour into martini glasses, set. Serve w sour cream & peeled, finely-diced cucumber on top.

Christine Hamilton, television presenter, journalist, *Celebrity Masterchef* contestant & self-styled 'Media Butterfly'.

L ⏲

Cambozola Figs *@gardenfix*
Stuff fresh figs w slices of Cambozola cheese. Instant sophistication.

L V

Boursin Buttons *@helen_kara*
Take wee button mushrooms, clean, remove stalks. Scrape out as much of gills as poss. Fill w Boursin. Scoff.

L V

Chillies In Chocolate *@helen_kara*
Slit fresh red chillies & deseed. Stuff & coat thickly w melted dark chocolate. Chill. Eat w chilled vodka if brave.

L

Posh Peppadew *@helen_kara*
Drain Peppadew peppers. Fill w plain or flavoured cream cheese. Put on cocktail sticks if feeling posh. Fiddly but worth it.

V L

Gorgonzola Canapés @MontanaGael
Wholewheat digestive biccies topped w Gorgonzola cheese, swirl of honey, ½ red grape each.

Prawn & Avocado Canapés @msmac
Mini toasts or bread crackers spread w red pesto. Top each w a prawn & sliver of avocado.

Cheats Blinis @Tracytid
Flatten bread w rolling pin, cut circles. Soak in melted butter&garlic, 180c till crisp. Top w salmon&cream cheese or mozzarella&tomato, etc.

Scotch Eggs @alisonwells
Hardboil egg, roll in flour. Cover in sausage meat, dip in beaten egg, roll in breadcrumbs. Deep fry, drain, serve.

Devilled Eggs @HOHWwriter
Boil egg. Cool, split. Pop out centre. Mix w mayo. Put back in cold white. Top w paprika.

Smoked Salmon Canapés @CountryLets
Slice baguette thinly, little OO. 180c till crisp. Top w cream cheese & smoked salmon, squeeze lemon & black pepper.

Stuffed Dates @MontanaGael
Stuff Medjool dates w sticks of Parmesan, wrap in prosciutto or bacon. Grill until cheese melts. Pop in mouth.

Crab Cocktail Canapés @deberryandgrant
2 packets cream cheese at room temp. Mix w 230g steamed (frozen/fresh) crab & 340g good cocktail sauce. Squeeze lemon. Serve w crackers.
Virginia Deberry & Donna Grant, bestselling authors of *What Doesn't Kill You.*

Baked Brie @DazedPuckBunny
Bake rindy wheel of brie on baking tray 180c 10 mins. Drizzle w fig balsamic vinegar. Decorate w strawberries, serve w toast.

Baked Camembert @SanyaV
Whole camembert in box (remove paper). S&P, grated orange rind, white wine on top. 200c 30-40mins till melted. Dunk sourdough bread. Share.

Deep-Fried Camembert @tcordrey
Cut chilled camembert into small wedges. Roll in egg & then breadcrumbs. Chill for 30 mins. Deep fry until very pale brown.

Roast Chicken Wings @goodtoweet
L
Toss chicken wings in EVOO & lemon juice. Sprinkle generously w ground chilli & salt. Roast 180c 30mins till crisp & golden.

Cheese Straws @helen_kara
V
Sheet puff pastry. Cover ½ w grated cheese & poppyseeds. Fold & roll, repeat, roll thin, cut strips, twist. Bake 180c 12-15mins.

L

Pigs In Blankets @JackyHSF
L
Wrap cocktail sausages lengthways in cheesy pastry. Brush w beaten egg. Bake 220c 12-15mins.

Individual Baked Potatoes @janetravers
V
Toss tiny Charlotte potatoes in OO, garlic. Sprinkle w sea salt, fresh rosemary. 180c 30 mins or till cooked through. Great finger food!

L

Crème Fraîche Baked Potatoes
@janetravers
V
Bake tiny Charlotte potatoes as above w OO & salt. Cut an X on top, squeeze to push out potato slightly. Top tsp crème fraîche & chives.

L

[L] Pesto Pinwheels @mduffywriter
Thinly roll readymade puff pastry. Spread w pesto & sprinkle w cheese. Roll, cut into thin slices. Spirals on baking sheet 160c 20mins.

[L] Sweet Snails @mduffywriter
Thinly roll out readymade puff pastry. Spread w jam. Roll up & cut into thin slices. Place spirals on baking sheet 160c 20 mins. [V]

[L] Goat's Cheese Tart @rosamundi
Ready-rolled puff pastry. Spread w pesto leaving 1cm edge all round. Scatter w goat's cheese & halved cherry toms/olives. Bake 200c 20mins.

> @rosamundi
> The above tart cut into squares makes great party nibbles.

[L] Filo Parcels @NettieWriter
Layer 3 filo pastry sheets w melted butter. Brie, bacon & cranberry sauce in middle. Twist to make parcel. Brush w melted butter. 180c 15 min.

[V] Garlic Bread @PenguinGalaxy
Chop garlic, spring onions & parsley small. Fry them in masses of butter. Pour into slits in bread! Bake 180c 8mins, eat! [L]

Drinks

Remember those old cartoons where an indecisive character had an angel sitting on one shoulder and a devil on the other, each whispering in his ear, each trying to guide him to see things their way? Well, this chapter will pose the same dilemma for you in written form!

In the first part of the chapter you'll find fantastic, healthy, vitamin- and antioxidant-packed juices and smoothies; in the second half you'll find alcohol, alcohol and more alcohol ... It's a perfect balance of yin and yang, black and white, good and bad – or maybe bad and good, depending on your perspective?

Oh yes, and tucked away at the end of the chapter are some handy cures for the morning after the night before. Enjoy!

Smoothies & Shakes

Live-To-Dance Shake @PaulaAbdul
Fresh kale, lettuce, cucumber, spinach, blueberries, peaches, kiwi, almond milk, stevia. Let it pirouette in blender till smooth.
Paula Abdul, American pop singer, dancer, choreographer, actress & television personality.

Spring Smoothie @fuelthefighter
1 scoop vanilla whey, 1 diced peach, 75g raspberries, 2tbsp honey crunch wheat germ, 125ml skim milk, 5 ice cubes. Blitz.

Apple Kale Lemon Smoothie @VitaDeals
4 apples (cored, skin on), handful kale leaves, ½ lemon (peeled), 375ml water, handful ice cubes, blender. Blitz for 1 min detox.

Fab Fruit Smoothie @GoBelfastMag
Blend 1 banana, handful frozen mixed berries, 1tsp honey, ½ lrg tub natural yogurt & a dash of orange juice.
GO Belfast, award-winning glossy magazine.

Peach Spinach Smoothie @VitaDeals
5 peaches, 12 spinach leaves, 375ml water, handful ice cubes, in blender. Blitz 1 min. YUM!

Supersmoothie @helen_kara
Juice 2 carrots, 2 apples, 2 oranges, 1 small lump root ginger. Blend 1 banana & 110g yogurt. Add juice & blend again.

Health Shake @CafeFresh
Blend together 2 bananas, handful of seeds, little apple juice & matcha tea powder. You'll be jumping around after this!

Sweet Lassi @NettieWriter
Whisk tog. large carton natural yogurt, ½ that quantity of milk, sugar to taste(1tbsp). Cools palate aft. spicy food.

Mango Lassi @HazelKLarkin
1 large mango (as ripe as poss – real Indian mangoes best), 250mls natural yogurt, little water if necessary, ice chips. Blend.

Iced Tea @BLNewport
6-8 small tea bags brought to boil in 2L water then add 2L of cold water. Add sugar before cold water so it dissolves. Ice & lemon.

@F414
Just don't steep iced tea too long, it should be golden brown, not halfway to espresso coffee colour. Add mint leaves & sugar.

Chocolat @joannechocolat
570mls milk. 5tbsp grated dark choc. Bring to boil. Add fresh chilli, brown sugar. Turn off heat. Serve. Perfect hot choc...

Joanne Harris, multi-award winning & best-selling author of *Chocolat*, judge of both the Whitbread & Orange prizes.

L V

Mexican Hot Chocolate @NettieWriter
Make a hot chocolate & add a cinnamon-stick stirrer. Arriba!!!

V

It's Happy Hour Again...

Rebus's Scotch Eggs @Beathhigh
Boil 2 free range eggs. Pour yourself a malt while you wait. Discard the eggs & keep drinking.

Ian Rankin, no. 1 best-selling crime author, creator of acclaimed *Inspector Rebus* series.

Smooth Simplicity @DonovanCreed
Recipe: Pour 4 ounces 20-year-old Pappy Van Winkle bourbon in a clean glass. Sip. (Who needs 140 characters?)

John Locke, American crime fiction writer of *Donovan Creed* books, first author to sell 1 million books on Kindle.

Gin Recipes

Best G&T @gardenfix
Broker's Gin, good tonic, ice, garnish w lime wedge, mint sprig, slice of cucumber. Pour mine soon!

California Gimlet @HackaPhreaka
2 parts gin, 1 part simple syrup, juice ½ lime. Lime wheel garnish. For simple syrup see page 146

London Iced Tea @HackaPhreaka
3 parts gin, 3 parts rum, 3 parts lemon juice, 2 parts amaretto, 2 parts simple syrup. Top up w coke. Lemon wedge garnish. For simple syrup see page 146

'Vesper Martini' @KFZuzulo
3 measures gin, 1 of vodka, half measure Kina Lillet/vermouth. Shake w ice till really cold & add thin slice lemon-peel. Get your Bond on :)
Kellyann Zuzulo, author of *The Genie's Curse* & others.

Beech Gin @honno
Fill a bottle w young beech leaves. Top up w gin, leave for 2 weeks. Strain, add sugar to taste. Drink!

Damson Gin @CountryLets
450g damsons, prick w fork. Put in 1L kilner jar. Add 170g sugar, top w gin. Shake each day until sugar dissolved. Cool dark place 3 months.

Vodka Recipes

Perfect End To The Day @LibertyLndnGirl
Vodka in freezer. Glass in one hand. Ice tongs in other. Drink.

Sasha Wilkins, English style journalist, editor & broadcaster, creator of multi-award winning lifestyle blog **LibertyLondonGirl**.

'Jane Austen Book Club' Martini @janeaustenworld
2 parts good vodka, 1 part fresh Key lime juice, 1 part Cointreau, splash of cranberry juice, lime wedge.

Classic Cranberry Martini @trendymartini
Vodka, orange liqueur, cranberry juice, fresh cranberry garnish.

White Russian @seo01
2 parts vodka, 1 part Kahlua, ice. In a small tumbler topped w cream or milk, a shake of cocoa to finish.

Black Russian @CountryLets
One part vodka, 3 parts coffee liqueur. Mix, serve.

Vodka Martini @janetravers
2 parts vodka, 1 part dry vermouth. Shake well w ice, strain into a cocktail glass. Garnish w an olive & serve.

Lychee Martini @JoTreggiari
Make a vodka martini, add lychee syrup & peeled lychee fruit skewered on a cocktail stick.
Jo Treggiari, author of children's book *Feltus Ovalton* & acclaimed teen novel *Ashes, Ashes*.

Cosmopolitan @charliedncn
2parts vodka, 1part Gr& Marnier/Cointreau, dash lime, dash cranberry. Shake over ice, strain & serve w slice of lime. Should be pink!

Rum

18th-Century Rum Punch @julianstockwin
My fave summer drink: 1 part sour (lime), 2 parts sweet (syrup), 3 parts strong (rum), 4 parts weak (water).
Julian Stockwin, best-selling author of the historical *Thomas Kydd* series.

Banana-Mango Daiquiri @SCallejo
1 mango, 1 banana, 60ml lime juice, 1tsp sugar syrup, 190ml white rum. Process fruit w juice & add syrup, rum & ice.

Mojitos @gardenfix
If mint's up, Mojitos: 2 parts rum, 2 parts club soda, 1 part lime juice, handful crushed fresh mint, 1tsp powdered sugar in a frosty glass.

Tequila

Bloody Jack @Keithpbarry
Jack Daniels mixed w a shot of tequila. Add half orange & half cranberry juice.

Keith Barry, magician & illusionist, internationally known on television & in theatres.

Margarita @F414
One part fresh lime juice, one part tequila, one part orange liquor. 2tsp sugar, salt on rim of glasses, ice cubes to taste.

Tequila Punch @GourmetRambler
500ml good silver tequila, 250ml Cointreau, 375ml fresh lime juice, 85ml simple syrup or to taste. Serve shaken on rocks, salted rim.

For simple syrup see page 146

Wine & Champagne

French 75 Champagne Cocktail @McGiff
In a champagne glass put a shot of gin, a squeeze of lemon juice. Top up w champagne, add a twist of lemon.
Carol McGiffen, English broadcaster & television personality, presenter on ITV's *Loose Women*, columnist for *Closer* magazine.

Werther's Bellini @AJHMurray
Try a Werther's Bellini – a Werther's Original in a glass of champagne. Surprisingly moreish.
Al Murray, Comedian & television personality of The Pub Landlord fame.

Chocolate Orange @twicipetweet
Large wine glass, fill w ice, double Tia Maria, top up w orange juice.

Kir @HackaPhreaka
Glass of white wine, splash of crème de cassis, lemon twist garnish.

Punch @rachspan
1 bottle red wine, 1 sliced lemon, 1 sliced orange, 2-3tbsp sugar, 1 shot brandy, 1 shot triple sec. Chill. Add 500ml gingerale, ice.

All A Writer Needs @janewenhamjones
Open bottle of wine, undo bar of chocolate. Empty both down throat. Mmmm. That's better :-)
Jane Wenham Jones, freelance writer, novelist & author of *Wannabe a Writer?*

Other Cocktails

Caipirinha @charliedncn
Tumbler glass, ½ lime in wedges, 2tsp sugar, smush together w crushed ice. Add large shot of cachaça, stir & serve.

Snowball @CountryLets
1 measure of Advocaat, 2 measures lemonade, squeeze of lime juice. Stir, top w cocktail cherry.

And for the Morning After the Night Before ... Hangover Cures!

Hangover Cure @janewenhamjones
Butter toast, add peanut butter topped w marmite & serve w lemon tea plus nurofen. Should this fail, add hair of dog.
Jane Wenham Jones, freelance writer, novelist & author of *Wannabe a Writer?*

Kill Or Cure @CafeFresh
Wheatgrass shot w 1000mg vitamin C added. Sit, drink & take a few deep breaths – kill or cure!

Fresh Fruit Smoothie Hangover Cure
@CafeFresh

Blend watermelon, orange juice, pineapple & mint. Add a spoon of natural yogurt. Drink!

Tea & Sympathy *@CountryLets*

Tea w honey in it! Caffeine reduces the dilated blood vessels causing headache & fructose from honey rids alcohol.

Easy Eggs *@CountryLets*

Eggs – fried, poached, boiled however you like them. Albumin in eggs help rehydrate cells alcohol has dehydrated.

Wodehouse Special *@LevParikian*

Raw egg, Worcestershire sauce, red pepper, clam juice, tabasco. Good enough for Jeeves, good enough for me.

Classic Cure *@Tracytid*

Bacon & egg sandwich w brown sauce, isotonic drink, dark glasses, lots of promises to self never to drink again.

Cooking Tips from Marco Pierre White

I've been asked many times for top kitchen tips. In my opinion there are three of them:

1. Use a great knife made from good-quality steel together with a large, thick chopping board. Using a good sharp knife made from steel that holds its edge is important. It does the work for you. You cut yourself with blunt knives, not with sharp knives.

2. Use great-quality, heavy pans. Cast iron frying pans or griddle pans are great to cook with because they conduct heat efficiently and retain it.

3. Use the best-quality ingredients that you can get.

If you do these three things, then you can achieve great results in the kitchen.

Marco Pierre White

'Food Inspired by the Movies' Quiz

• • • • • • • • • • • • • • • • •

When I was gathering the recipes for *Tweet Treats*, I set a different 'keyword challenge' every day to help spark tweeters' ideas. One day I suggested 'food from the movies', which produced some very inventive recipes. See if you can guess the movies these tweets refer to (answers at the bottom).

1. @neversarah Stew (Rainier) cherries; bake in a pie. Serve with a damn fine cup of coffee.

2. @LevParikian Ingredients: 1 sausage, 1 Camberwell carrot, 1 hare (here) and the finest wines known to humanity.

3. @janetravers Combine greek yogurt and a swirl of honey. Top with chopped nuts. Now eat with your fingers, cos there is no spoon.

4. @thejayfaulkner Fry onion,pepper,aubergine, courgette,garlic.Add tomatoes,sage,rosemary,oregano, S&P. Add 2 rats.

5. @mduffywriter Spray some oil on oven tray & line with veg. Ask Angela to put it in the oven. Angela goes shopping.

6. @rebeccaebrown Find a large watermelon. Put it in a corner.

7. @HazelKLarkin Take a cocoa confection of your choice. Unwrap. Dip in coffee if desired. Nibble. Enjoy.

8. @rebeccaebrown Tie asparagus stalks with blue string and make into soup.

9. @thejayfaulkner Find coconut. Cut coconut. Eat coconut. Repeat until rescued ... or dead.

10. @janetravers Combine wrens' livers, larks' tongues, ocelots' noses and badgers' spleens. Eat. You're a very naughty boy.

Answers:

1. Twin Peaks 2. Withnail and I 3. The Matrix 4. Ratatouille 5. Angela's Ashes 6. Dirty Dancing 7. Chocolat 8. Bridget Jones' Diary 9. Castaway 10. The Life Of Brian

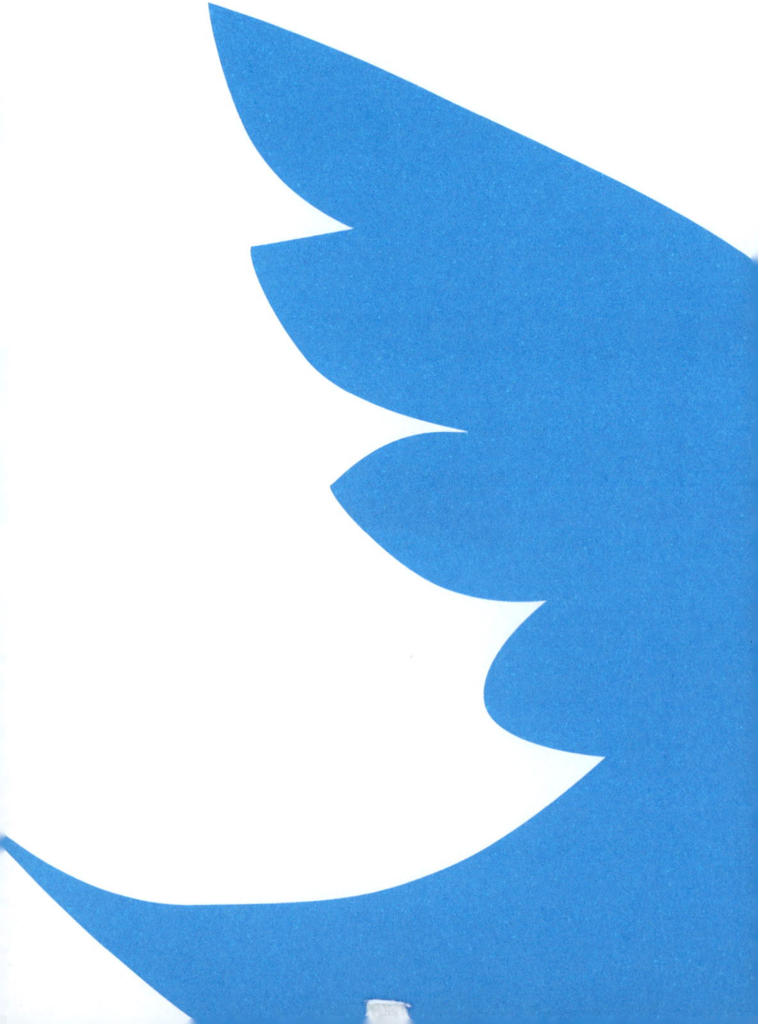

Turn the page for more great cookbooks from

O'BRIEN

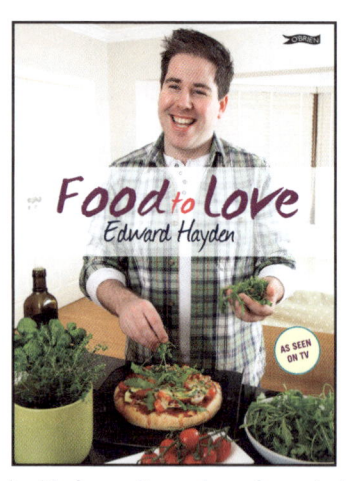

Packed with favourite recipes for salads, soups, one-pot wonders, versatile main courses, chutneys & relishes, delicious, crusty breads, al fresco dining suggestions, festive foods, tempting, finger-licking desserts and gorgeous cakes and bakes – this truly is food to love.

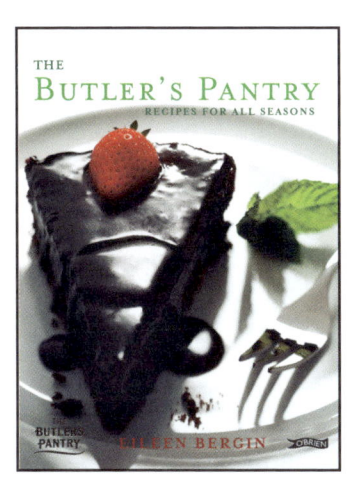

Divided into the four seasons – plus Christmas – this book provides mouth-watering recipes based on the best ingredients available for starters main courses, desserts and snacks!

Also included are tips on getting started in the kitchen, the most useful ingredients to have in your cupboard, and catering for friends.

A selection of mouth-watering and unusual soups from Ireland – including wild garlic and potato, cream of wild salmon, Maire Rua soup made from fresh beetroot, patriot soup, pea and ham, roast plum and red cabbage. Interesting morsels of information on Irish folklore and tradition enhance the recipes.

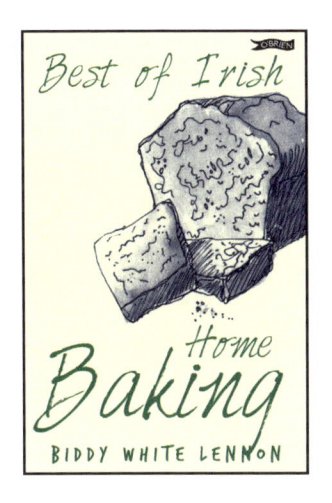

These sixty tempting recipes include soda breads, potato and griddle breads, gur cake, porter cake, barm brack and Christmas cake, buttermilk scones, pancakes, puddings and oaten biscuits. They will delight visitors and Irish people alike. Details of customs, folklore and Irish regional food traditions provide a fascinating background to the recipes and forty charming illustrations complete the mix.

Best of Irish Traditional Cooking

BIDDY WHITE LENNON

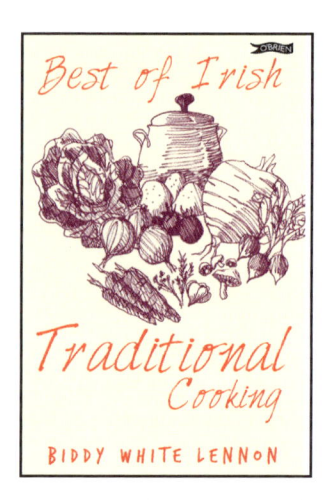

From starters to puddings, you will find a delicious selection of recipes using the best of Irish ingredients: succulent salmon, creamy cheeses, nutty brown flour. Choose from Bantry Bay mussels, Dublin Coddle, Kerry apple cakes, Guinness stew, Baileys cheesecake and of course the famous Irish Coffee.

The potato has long been a staple of the Irish diet. Here, Biddy White Lennon gathers together some of the best recipes based on the humble potato. With flavours ranging from sweet to spicy, savoury to sumptuous, Biddy brings out the best in this versatile vegetable.

The Irish have many days for feasting and traditional celebration: St Brigid's Day, St Patrick's Day, Shrove Tuesday, Bealtaine, Bloomsday, Lughnasa, Hallowe'en, Women's Christmas (Nollaig na mBan). Then there are the newer festivals that celebrate the rich harvest of our seas and fields. These sixty recipes offer a tempting selection of foods for all these occasions.

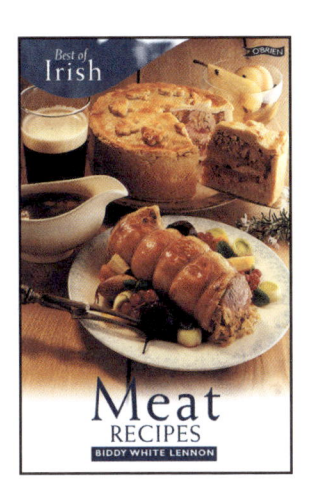

Fifty inspiring recipes featuring beef, lamb, pork, poultry, game, and dishes using cured, spiced and smoked meats. There are traditional dishes such as Irish stew, Michaelmas roast goose, bacon and cabbage; local specialities like Cork crubeens and Dingle pies.

www.obrien.ie